Cambridge Elements

Elements in Magic
edited by
Marion Gibson
University of Exeter

STAGING WITCHCRAFT BEFORE THE LAW

Skepticism, Performance as Proof, and Law as Magic in Early Modern Witch Trials

Julie Stone Peters
Columbia University

CAMBRIDGE
UNIVERSITY PRESS

Shaftesbury Road, Cambridge CB2 8EA, United Kingdom

One Liberty Plaza, 20th Floor, New York, NY 10006, USA

477 Williamstown Road, Port Melbourne, VIC 3207, Australia

314–321, 3rd Floor, Plot 3, Splendor Forum, Jasola District Centre, New Delhi – 110025, India

103 Penang Road, #05–06/07, Visioncrest Commercial, Singapore 238467

Cambridge University Press is part of Cambridge University Press & Assessment, a department of the University of Cambridge.

We share the University's mission to contribute to society through the pursuit of education, learning and research at the highest international levels of excellence.

www.cambridge.org
Information on this title: www.cambridge.org/9781009469708

DOI: 10.1017/9781009469692

First published 2024

A catalogue record for this publication is available from the British Library

ISBN 978-1-009-46970-8 Hardback
ISBN 978-1-009-46971-5 Paperback
ISSN 2732-4087 (online)
ISSN 2732-4079 (print)

Staging Witchcraft before the Law

Skepticism, Performance as Proof, and Law as Magic in Early Modern Witch Trials

Elements in Magic

DOI: 10.1017/9781009469692
First published online: December 2024

Julie Stone Peters
Columbia University

Author for correspondence: Julie Stone Peters, peters@columbia.edu

Abstract: While the judicial machinery of early modern witch-hunting could work with terrifying swiftness, skepticism and evidentiary barriers often made conviction difficult. Seeking proof strong enough to overcome skepticism, judges and accusers turned to performance, staging "acts of Sorcery and Witch-craft manifest to sense." Looking at an array of demonological treatises, pamphlets, documents, and images, this Element shows that such staging answered to specific doctrines of proof: catching the criminal "in the acte"; establishing "notoriety of the fact"; producing "violent presumptions" of guilt. But performance sometimes overflowed the demands of doctrine, behaving in unpredictable ways. A detailed examination of two cases – the 1591 case of the French witch-demoniac Françoise Fontaine and the 1593 case of John Samuel of Warboys – suggests the manifold, multilayered ways that evidentiary staging could signify, – as it can still in that conjuring practice we call law. This title is also available as Open Access on Cambridge Core.

This Element also has a video abstract: www.cambridge.org/EMGI_Peters

Keywords: witchcraft, law, performance, skepticism, proof, staging, evidence, magic, the senses, possession

ISBNs: 9781009469708 (HB), 9781009469715 (PB), 9781009469692 (OC)
ISSNs: 2732-4087 (online), 2732-4079 (print)

Contents

1 Introduction

This Element explores a set of extraordinary episodes during early modern witch trials: those moments in which judges, petty magistrates, accusers, victims, or the alleged witches themselves staged or performed witchcraft as evidence of the crime. In courtrooms, examination chambers, prisons, and public spaces for gathering evidence, seeking proof by whatever means they could, participants ordered the accused to conjure the devil or devil's familiars, create hailstorms, or turn themselves into wolves. They brought bewitched "demoniacs" before juries and witnesses, where the victims fell into fits: spoke in demonic voices, thrashed with palsy-like shakes, turned their bodies into hoops, howled like dogs on their hands and knees, found themselves elevated in the air or dragged by invisible hands across the courtroom floor, vomited hair, straw, or nails. Authorities – sometimes self-appointed – tested victims to determine whether they were truly bewitched: poking them with pins, burning their hands, whipping them with rods. They took up traditional remedies as evidentiary devices: scratching the witch, burning thatch from her roof, or casting the name of the devil and perfumes into the fire. They chanted counter-diabolical spells to expel animal demons and relieve the victim of her torments, and watched as the devil thrashed and cried out from her body. They made the invisible world visible and set it in motion.[1]

Early modern witch trials never cease to fascinate scholars and general readers. How could so many have believed that the world was peopled by witches? Why did so many confess? How could so many innocent people have been tortured and judicially murdered? The result has been hundreds of books on early modern witchcraft and the witch trials. And yet there is still

[1] Gendered pronouns here reflect the fact that the accused and alleged victims were mostly female, but many were male, as my examples will suggest. For orders to perform magic, see e.g. Phillips, *Examination*, sig. A7v (conjure devils or familiars in the courtroom); Institoris, *Hammer*, 559 (create a hailstorm); Boguet, *Discours des sorciers*, 121 (turn themselves into wolves). For fits before juries or witnesses, see e.g. *Most Wonderfull and True Storie*, 34–5 (demonic voices); *Most Strange and Admirable Discoverie*, sig. A3r (palsy-like shakes); Bradwell, "Mary Glovers," 5 (turning bodies into hoops); Boguet, *Discours des sorciers*, 142 (howling like dogs on hands and knees); Bénet, *Procès verbal*, 27–8 (elevated in air and dragged across floor); Cotta, *Triall*, 76 (vomiting hair, straw, or nails). For tests, see e.g. Bradwell, "Mary Glovers," 21 (poking with pins and burning hands); Baddeley, *Boy of Bilson*, 32 (whipping with rods). For traditional remedies as evidence, see e.g. *Most Strange and Admirable Discoverie*, sig. B2r–v (scratching); Galis, *Brief Treatise*, sig. D1r (burning thatch); Boguet, *Discours des sorciers*, 148 (casting name of devil and perfumes into fire). For counter-diabolical spells and watching the devil cry out from the victim's body, see e.g. *Most Wonderfull and True Storie*, 34–5. These are merely a few instances of such recurrent performance tropes.

A note on texts: all translations are my own except where I cite published translations. In transcriptions, I modernize only the letters u, v, i, j, and s and eliminate ligatures. In translations – as in quotes originally in English – I use brackets to indicate substantial changes, such as modification of number or tense.

much to be discovered, not only by uncovering new documents or data but also by highlighting things that historians of the trials have largely ignored.

Historians tend to address the trials in one of two ways: either they focus on individual panics, looking closely at the particulars of social history; or they address broadscale questions, trying to understand how demography, economics, geography, religious conflict, or other social forces contributed to the witch hunts. Legal historians generally focus on the central operative juridical concepts and procedures that made convictions possible. Literary scholars and scholars of visual culture typically look at representations of the trials in texts or images, seeking to understand how rhetoric, narrative, and aesthetic norms shaped ideas about witchcraft.

My Element differs from these in a number of respects. As a cultural historian, I am interested in broad historical questions, but I seek to understand them primarily through their expression in embodied, material, sensory forms. As a scholar of literature and visual culture, I am interested in representation, but my focus is not on textual or visual representation *of* events (like most such scholarship), but on the events themselves *as* representations.[2] Looking at the staging of trials – at on-the-ground scenes as they unfolded through gesture, action, and speech – I am interested in what the participants did, said, and meant and what those present saw, heard, understood, and felt. My attention is not just on what happened and how it happened but on the event as a mode of collective meaning-making. I am particularly concerned with events bounded in local space and time, staged for spectators and speaking to sensory perception in the here and now: what we can call, for lack of a better word, "performance."

Early modern texts had various ways of describing the thing we call "performance," often using theatrical terms: they were "spectacle[s]," "Scene[s]," "pageantes," "play[s]," or (for the skeptic Samuel Harsnett) "tragicall Comedie[s]."[3] In the witch trials (as in other contexts), the word "performance" sometimes referred to actions that entailed precisely the kind of visible display before audiences that we associate with performance: the bewitched Mary Glover "advanc[ed] . . . her body as though she would daunce: [and] [t]hen did she performe very nimble and strange motions of her hands, and fingers,"

[2] In trying to distinguish events from textual or visual representations, I am especially indebted to Marion Gibson's detailed analysis of the value and risks of using pamphlets as historical sources, and her discussion of methodologies for doing so: particularly the introductions and notes in *Early Modern Witches* and *Reading Witchcraft* (especially 49–74), but also *Witches of St Osyth* (especially 216–18); and *Rediscovering Renaissance Witchcraft*, 6–24. While striving throughout to maintain a healthy skepticism about the veracity of the pamphlets, I also seek to uncover in them clues to what actually happened. For more detailed discussion of my historical methodology, see my "Law as Performance"; and *Law as Performance*, 21–3.

[3] For "spectacle," see *Most Wonderfull and True Storie*, 24; for "pageantes," Phillips, *Examination*, sig. A3r; for "Scene" and "tragicall Comedie," Harsnett, *Discovery*, 142.

first "as though she had an harpe, then as though she had a payer of virginalls before her."[4]

In my recent book, *Law as Performance*, I say more about what I mean by "performance" and "spectatorship" and why we should view these as crucial means of producing, disseminating, and experiencing law.[5] There, investigating the long history of legal performance and spectatorship in Europe, I identify the importance of performance – as both a set of practices and a concept – to law. I argue not only that law was produced in part through performance, but that the conceptual opposition between law and theatrics was constitutive for law, defining it through its antithesis with theater.

This Element is at once an offshoot of that book and quite different from it. *Law as Performance* reaches across the *longue durée*, tracing a tradition of thought and practice as it appeared in different guises in ancient, medieval, and early modern Europe. This study, on the contrary, focuses on a fairly circumscribed period (primarily c. 1580–1620) in order to examine a specific constellation of historical effects.[6] Where the book looked at performance and spectatorship generally, this Element focuses especially on staging: that is, on intentional practices with clear legal aims. In the book, witch trials appear only briefly (and a century earlier than the period I treat here): in my discussion of the Innsbruck trial of 1485 and the struggle between inquisitor Heinrich Institoris (aka Kramer) and a feisty defendant named Helena Scheuberin.[7] Here, of course, witch trials take center stage. Moreover, here I focus on a crucial issue to which I give virtually no attention in the book: how performance served proof.

Performance may not seem like a new concern for studies of witchcraft. After all, scholars have looked at performance in plays about witches, in the practice of witchcraft, and in the scenes of possession that a number of prominent studies have explored.[8] Studies sometimes note the theatricality of early modern narrative and pictorial representations of witchcraft: the wild dancing to cacophonous music at witches' sabbats; the performance of magic and conjuring of

4 Bradwell, "Mary Glovers," 7. 5 Peters, *Law as Performance*, 17–19.

6 I have restricted myself to evidence almost solely from this period in order to emphasize the fact that the skepticism at the heart of my argument was not a late seventeenth-century phenomenon but key to the trials at their height. But there are, in fact, many later seventeenth-century instances of staging-as-proof in response to skepticism. See e.g. Hopkins, *Discovery*, 2, 5–6 (1644 trials); *Tryal of Witches*, 2, 42–7 (1662 trial), and North, *Life of the Right Honourable Francis North*, 131–2 (trial in the 1670s). These are just three of many examples.

7 Peters, *Law as Performance*, 176–85.

8 On the relationship between historic witch trials and theatrical spectacle in such plays as *Doctor Faustus*, *The Witch of Edmonton*, or *The Late Lancashire Witches*, see e.g. Deats, "'Mark This Show'"; and Coffin, "Theatre and/as Witchcraft." Influential studies that have stressed the theatricality of witch trials, possession cases, and exorcisms include, most notably, Certeau, *Possession*; Greenblatt, "Loudun" and "Shakespeare"; and Levack, *Devil Within*.

visions. But even when such studies look specifically at trials, they tend to focus not on events that actually took place before the law but on events elsewhere: a neighbor's curse, diabolical spell, or night flight described in a trial account; the social and conceptual world of witch beliefs that accusations and confessions reveal. That is, when they attend to theatricality, they treat it almost solely as a narrative effect.[9] Scholars do sometimes reference the "social performance of witchcraft," but usually only peripherally or to make a broad historical claim about witchcraft as a "cultural drama."[10] In short, where such studies leave off, I begin.

Virginia Krause has argued that the regime of the trials (in France at least) was an "auricular regime": that the ear had become "the privileged portal for sacred truths," that witchcraft "could be heard but not seen." Certainly, the "audible invisibility" she describes was crucial to belief: confessions, curses, cries, mysterious sounds.[11] But so was visibility: witchcraft enacted before the eyes of spectators.[12] My principal goal is not to argue *that* performance mattered to witch trials (though that it did should become clear in the course of my discussion) but to show *how* it worked, both legally and expressively. I look at trials as events: how witnesses and the accused behaved before judges; what judges, juries, and trial audiences saw and heard. To understand evidentiary performance requires trying to envision details of staging, the use of space, the production of conceptual, sensory, and affective experience, the multiple and contradictory forms of visual and auditory sense-making. It requires delving into the moment-by-moment experience of the event, looking at evidence as it

---

9 An exception is Laura Levine's *Afterlives of Endor*, which appeared when my Element was already in production. While she dedicates much of her book to literary texts, her concern with performance in the pamphlet and four treatises she analyzes dovetails with my own.

10 See e.g. Roper, *Oedipus and the Devil* (in confession, a woman could "translat[e] her own life experiences into the language of the diabolic, performing her own diabolic theatre" [19]; exorcism "involved the battle of spiritual forces in the theatre of the body itself" [42]); Roper, *Witch Craze*, 75 (one confession was "a performance of venomous bravura"); Dolan, *True Relations* (pamphlets shaped the "social performance of witchcraft" [67]); Witmore, *Pretty Creatures* (pamphlets were "scripts" for performing possession [181]); Levack, "Possession" (Anne Gunter's performances of bewitchment were "the main theatrical attraction in Oxford" [1622]); Levack, *Devil Within* (possession was a ritual [especially 139–68]); Almond, *Demonic Possession* (possession was a "cultural drama" played "within the confines of a cultural script" [ix]); Butler, "Bedeviling Spectacle" (calling for further examination of performance in witch trials).

11 Krause, *Witchcraft*, 4; and see 44–72.

12 This Element does not challenge Krause's claim but serves as a necessary supplement to it. My arguments do stand in tension with Holger Syme's claim that spectacular displays were not authoritative forms of evidence in English witch trials (*Theatre and Testimony*, 209–21). The difference may lie in the narrowness of Syme's definition of the "authoritative," which excludes (for instance) evidence displayed to a jury only briefly, produced only in judges' chambers, staged by judges ambivalent about its value, or not serving as "centrepieces" of a trial (214). But he does recognize that demoniacs regularly performed their fits in the courtroom for evidentiary purposes (219).

unfolds in time. For evidence does not consist in a collection of static objects. It emerges as a process rather than a set of products. Like a story, it can be full of surprises, plot twists, reversals.

This project may appear very different from mainstream legal history in its attention to staging: to the sensory, kinesthetic, and affective; to aesthetics generally. But it dovetails with the concerns of more traditional legal historians in its concern with doctrine, specifically certain evidentiary doctrines that the history of evidence has largely overlooked.[13] Because witch trials are conventionally portrayed as unconstrained in their brutality, readers tend to assume that there were no rules of evidence constraining judgment. This is not in fact the case. It is true that the modern law of evidence (with its detailed rules of admissibility) did not develop until the eighteenth century, and that judges and juries were often oblivious to evidentiary doctrine, simply concluding what they wanted to conclude. But demonologists and civil law judges regularly cited Roman-canon law rules of proof, and English common law judges often called on these when instructing juries.[14]

As I will show, staging in legal arenas answered to three early modern evidentiary doctrines: taking "*in flagrante*"; showing the "*notorietas facti*" ("notoriety of the fact"); and recognizing *indicia indubitata* ("violent presumptions" of guilt). While the doctrines sometimes appeared in formal legal language (in the work of jurists and demonologists), they more often appeared in what we might call "the doctrinal vernacular": doctrinal ideas that have trickled down into the collective consciousness, transformed into general assumptions about innocence and guilt, exoneration and proof. Thus, when judges or accusers worked to stage proof, they were not necessarily drawing explicitly on formal doctrine. They were often instead drawing on common assumptions that flowed from these doctrines.

Legal historians tend to segregate English common law from civil (largely Roman) law and canon law.[15] But as demonological treatises and reports of witchcraft circulated around Europe, so did the legal doctrines they conveyed, among them the three doctrines of proof I have identified. These had purchase not only on the Continent and in Scotland but in England as well. While continental jurists were mostly ignorant of English common law, there was

---

13 The doctrines I look at appear only peripherally in the few existing studies of early modern evidence. These include (most notably) Langbein, *Torture*; and (for general discussions of Roman-canon rules of proof), Rosoni, *Quae singula*; and Damaška, *Evaluation*.

14 For brief discussions of evidence and procedure in continental witch trials, see Schlaefli, *Procès de sorcellerie*, 11–22; Ankarloo, Clark, and Monter, *Witchcraft and Magic*, 7–10, 64–99; and Homza, *Village Infernos*, 87–121. For discussions of evidence in English witch trials, see Darr, *Marks of an Absolute Witch*; Gaskill, "Witchcraft and Evidence"; Holmes, "Women: Witnesses and Witches"; Durston, *Witchcraft*, 391–419; and Shapiro, "*Beyond Reasonable Doubt*," 194–226 (and throughout on seventeenth-century ideas of evidence generally).

15 For both diagnosis and refutation of this position (addressing the alleged split around the thirteenth century), see Kamali, "Finding Facts in Medieval English Law."

a certain traffic between Scottish civil law and English common law, and English jurists were deeply interested in civil and canon law generally. These were not, of course, solely foreign curiosities. English ecclesiastical law was derived from Catholic canon law. Civil law was the only kind that the Oxford and Cambridge law faculties taught. And many graduates of these faculties went on to serve in the English civil and ecclesiastical law courts.[16] If English jurists were at pains to identify the distinctiveness of the common law, they were also at pains to draw parallels between the common law and civil law. In demonological treatises, they called attention not only to the universal biblical foundations of the penalty for witchcraft but also to ideas about probability and methods of proof that they shared with their Scottish and continental counterparts.[17]

The concept of probability could serve claims about certainty, but it could also, of course, serve claims about doubt. While historians of the trials have long recognized the importance of skepticism throughout the period of the trials and its deep roots in church doctrine, skepticism still often appears as an Enlightenment phenomenon in the popular imagination, heralding the end of the trials.[18] Certainly, skepticism played a role in ending the trials and could serve as a brake on prosecutions. But (as I argue), it also often drove prosecutions, inspiring true believers with a zeal for proving the witch's guilt. Virtually all of the demonological treatises – many of them by judges dedicated to the extermination of witches – make it clear that their central *raison d'être* is the necessity of refuting skepticism. Judges similarly designed trials that would not merely eradicate witchcraft but *demonstrate* its dangers to skeptics.

To answer the skeptics, one needed dramatically spectacular proof. Like witch trials themselves, such spectacular proof may have been relatively rare, for it was hard to get the accused – or even accusers – to perform on cue. Many continental judges followed the rule that witnesses were to be interrogated only behind closed doors, protected by a veil of secrecy.[19] Sometimes the only public event was the reading of a judgment at a public sentencing and the execution of the judgment. But in England, trials in the secular courts were open to the public, and on the Continent and in Scotland, despite Roman-canon law norms, trials could in fact

[16] See Peters, *Law as Performance*, 252–3, 266 (and Ch. 6 generally on civil law education in England).

[17] See Shapiro, *Probability*, especially 194–226, but also 163–93; Klotz, "Suspicion," 1–70; and on early modern probability theory generally, Campe, *Game*, 15–36. For a slightly later period, see Daston, *Classical Probability*, 296–369.

[18] On skepticism, see e.g. Clark, *Thinking With Demons*, 195–213 and "'Feigned Deities'"; Stephens, *Demon Lovers* and "Sceptical Tradition"; Duni, "Skepticism"; Quensel, *Witch Politics*, 583–642. While Stephens's argument about the demonologists' need to answer skepticism is close to mine, his focus is mostly on verbal attestation rather than proof enacted in the courtroom.

[19] For useful discussions of criminal trial procedures on the Continent, see e.g. Langbein, *Prosecuting Crime*; Boes, *Crime and Punishment*; and Stern, *Criminal Law System*.

be very public events as well. There, officials often held pretrial investigations publicly. Even closed trials could take place before numerous observers, sometimes with spectators watching through courtroom windows.[20] Witch trials – perhaps more than any other kind of trial – attracted large audiences. "[F]ive hundred men" allegedly came to see accused witch Agnes Samuel bewitch Joan Throckmorton at the Huntington Assizes in 1593.[21] Mary Spencer, one of the accused at the 1633 Lancaster Assize trials, claimed that "the throng [was] so great that she could not hear the evidence against her."[22]

Even where a judge interrogated the accused alone in his chambers, visible presence and embodied communication – gestures, facial expressions, the expression of emotion – could be crucial forms of evidence.[23] These were all the more essential where others were present. Judges, juries, and spectators attempted to analyze the movements of the accused and watch their faces and bodies for telltale signs: Was the accused unable to shed tears? Did she keep her gaze fixed on the ground? (Sure signs of a witch.)[24] Intense emotional dramas could unfold in the courtroom or interrogation chambers: the accused might fall to their knees begging, throw themselves face down on the ground, tear their hair, attack their accusers. And sometimes – as in the moments I describe at the beginning of this Element – witches, the bewitched, or others in the courtroom performed witchcraft, proved its power, or revealed its secrets before the assembled judges and spectators.

These moments, however extraordinary, were common enough to produce something like a repertoire of early modern witch trial performance conventions: a performative poetics, bodily rhetoric, set of performance tropes or "theatregrams."[25] These were transmitted across borders through pamphlet literature, word-of-mouth, and live spectatorship itself. Among them were what Philip Almond has referred to as the "grammar" of demonic possession: thrashing, palsy-like shakes, swelling of the belly, trances, the impression of bodily weight, speaking in demonic voices, engaging in dialogue with invisible

[20] For examples, see Bénet, *Procès*, 68; Boguet, *Procès inédits*, 17; and Peters, *Law as Performance*, 13–15 (and, on large audiences at continental trials generally, 11–17, 92–3, 110–11, 119, 150–76, 200–4, 228–32, 238–50).

[21] *Most Strange and Admirable Discoverie*, sig. N3v (and see my discussion of the case in Section 4). For a discussion of audience, spatial configurations, and the concept of the "open court," see Mukherji, *Law and Representation*, 174–205; and Peters, *Law as Performance*, 11, 205, 227–32. On additional evidence of crowds at English witch trials and assizes generally, see e.g. Potts, *Wonderfull Discoverie*, sig. B1r; Aubrey, *Remaines*, 261; and Graham, *Ordering Law*, 45, 57.

[22] *Calendar of State Papers* (1634–5), 79; quoted in Sharpe, "Women," 113.

[23] On emotion in witch trials, see Kounine and Ostling, *Emotions*; Kounine, *Imagining*; and Millar, *Witchcraft*.

[24] For classic statements of these continental truisms, see Institoris, *Hammer*, 549–50; and Boguet, *Discours des sorciers*, 102. The claim about tears was less common in England, but see Bernard, *Guide*, 239.

[25] See Clubb, *Italian*, 6, for the useful term "theatregrams."

and inaudible familiars, and more.[26] Among them were also certain performance practices specific to witch trials: practices that served the specifically legal and evidentiary function of making "acts of Sorcery and Witch-craft manifest to sense" (as one demonologist put it).[27]

In identifying the repertoire of early modern witch trial performance conventions and arguing that these answered to the three specific evidentiary doctrines I discuss (as I do in greater detail in Section 2 of this Element), I have sought to reveal a structural-normative relationship between staging and doctrine. However, this relationship was, in practice, far more complex than my initial schema might suggest. If doctrine demanded specific kinds of proof and staging conventions sometimes obliged, they also sometimes failed to do so. As I argue in Sections 3 and 4, while ostensibly serving evidentiary functions, performances often went rogue, exceeding the intentions of their stagers, generating expressive effects and meanings that overflowed the demands of doctrine and were as complex, layered, variable, and contradictory as those to be found in texts. Sections 3 and 4 attempt to represent some of the complexity of such meaning-making through the close examination of two cases: the virtually unstudied case of the alleged witch and demoniac Françoise Fontaine in Louviers, France in 1591; and a well-known episode in the trial of the witches of Warboys at the Huntington Assizes in England in 1593.

2 Performance as Proof of the "Hidden Crime"

2.1 The Problem of Proving the "Hidden Crime"

Looking at the death toll from the mass witch hunts of the sixteenth and seventeenth centuries, and at the period's inflamed rhetoric attacking witches, it is easy to forget how comparatively rare executions for witchcraft were in most places in early modern Europe.[28] Authorities often decided not to prosecute, and trials often resulted in acquittal, as those dedicated to eradicating witchcraft routinely complained. Accusers found that it could be hard to convict a witch. For "full proof" in criminal cases, Roman civil and canon law (governing most of continental Europe, Scotland, and some English courts) normally required two credible eyewitnesses or a voluntary confession. Some judges

[26] Almond, *Demonic Possession*, 2. [27] Cotta, *Triall*, 84.

[28] Historians now generally agree that, except during the worst witch-hunting epidemics, accusations rarely led to indictments, and where they did, acquittals were more common than guilty verdicts. See Gaskill, "Witchcraft and Evidence," 40–2, Sharpe, *Bewitching*, 118, and Levack, "Possession," 1624 (on England); Maxwell-Stuart, *Witchcraft*, 72–3 (on Scotland); de Waardt, "Witchcraft," 242–6 (on the Netherlands); Pearl, *Crime*, 33 (on France). Even in Germany, where the most extreme witch hunts took place, courts were usually relatively restrained, and German regions with large-scale witch hunts were in fact the exception rather than the norm (Briggs, *Witches*; Rowlands, *Witchcraft*, 2; Kounine, *Imagining*, 7).

required that supplementary evidence confirm a confession. Despite the fact that there were technically no evidentiary rules under English common law (since the jury was the decider), common law judges and manuals on the prosecution of witchcraft often cited the Roman-canon law rule and its biblical corollary: "One witnesse shall not rise against a man for any trespasse, or for any sinne, or for any fault that he offendeth in, *but* at the mouth of two witnesses or at the mouth of three witnesses."[29] English judges often directed juries to be cautious, specifying the kind of evidence needed to convict. Even demonologists who passionately championed witch-hunting could argue that judges or juries must not convict on "bare presumptions, without sound and sufficient proofes," as William Perkins writes in his *Discourse of the Damned Art of Witchcraft* (c. 1590–9).[30] Even some of the most ardent crusaders against witchcraft might "mak[e] conscience to accuse [a witch] till it appeared upon sure proofe."[31]

The problem with witchcraft was that it was a "hidden crime" (as everyone knew), performed in secret, usually at night.[32] Many courts treated witchcraft as a *crimen exceptum*: not only an exceptionally heinous crime but exceptionally difficult to prove. In a *crimen exceptum*, they argued, the judge could relax evidentiary rules: those prohibiting torture without probable cause, barring certain kinds of witnesses (notably, felons and children), and prohibiting conviction on circumstantial evidence alone.[33] Even so, getting sure proof could be extraordinarily difficult: witnesses to the act itself were hard to find; witches did not always confess. The official prohibition on torture in England made it much harder to get confessions.[34] As Perkins writes, "the league with Satan is closely made, and the practises of Sorcerie are also very secret, and hardly can a man be brought [into court], which

---

29 Deuteronomy 19:15, *Bible Translated* (1592 Geneva Bible), fol. 79. Unless otherwise noted, all biblical references are to this edition, with biblical chapter and verse followed by folio number.

30 Perkins, *Discourse*, 218 (probably written in the 1590s though published only posthumously). See similarly Boguet: "en fact de crimes, le droit veut que les preuves soient plus claires, que le jour" (*Discours des sorciers,* 6 [*Examen*, 6]).

31 *Most Wonderfull and True Storie*, 5. For a discussion of the migration of the continental language of presumptions and proofs into English witchcraft jurisprudence, see Gaskill, "Witchcraft and Evidence," 68.

32 See e.g. Boguet, *Discours des sorciers*, 168 (*Examen*, 211).

33 On witchcraft as a *crimen exceptum* (a doctine not all courts accepted), see Larner, "Crimen Exceptum?"; Pearl, *Crime*, 33–4; Shapiro, "Classical Rhetoric," 69; and Goodare, *European Witch-Hunt*, 202. On the evidentiary exceptions that prosecuting a *crimen exceptum* allowed, see e.g. Institoris, *Malleus*, 198A–C (*Hammer*, 511–12); Del Río, *Disquisitiones*, 52–3 (Bk. 5, Sec. 6; *Investigations*, 210); Boguet, *Discours des sorciers*, 7, 131, 168, 184–5. And see Gaskill, "Witches and Witchcraft": English magistrates "were advised not to expect solid evidence for this most diabolical of crimes and instead to proceed using 'special presumptions'" (271). See Ankarloo, Clark, and Monter, *Witchcraft and Magic*, 7–10, 64–99, for examples of officials punished for violating rules of evidence and of accused witches released.

34 Torture was in fact often used in English treason cases, but not generally in English witch trials. See Heath, *Torture*.

upon his owne knowledge, can averre such things."[35] Witchcraft was *not* a crime "manifest to many eyes" or sometimes to "outward sense" at all, as the English physician-demonologist John Cotta complained in his *Triall of Witchcraft* (1616). "How," he asked, "is it possible that man can attaine any knowledge of [it?]"[36] It sometimes appears (sighed Perkins) virtually "impossible to put any one to death" for witchcraft.[37]

Richard Galis's *Brief Treatise Containing the Most Strange and Horrible Cruelty of Elizabeth Stile Alias Rockingham and her Confederates* (1579), describing his alleged persecution by four local Windsor witches, offers an extreme but nevertheless symptomatic example of the extraordinary lengths to which accusers sometimes went to prove witchcraft. Enraged at the magistrates for "winking" at the "devilish page[an]ts played" by the witches supposedly tormenting him, furious that "there was no Justice that would execute his office," Galis took the law into his own hands.[38] He determined to try the women himself: "proove [them] to be Witches" through various means and then "use [his] owne force upon them" (a measure that the inadequacy of judicial force seemed to justify). He would thus single-handedly "extirpat[e] and pul[l] up the saide wicked wéedes by the rootes" (sig. C2r–C4v). A series of tragicomic debacles followed. At one point, he entered one of the alleged witches' homes, bound a cart rope around her, and "forceably . . . pulled her out of her house" and down the street ("to the great astonishement of all the beholders") (Fig. 1). He brought her to the lodgings of the High Sheriff who, to Galis's indignation, let her go (sig. C3v–C4r). At another point, he dragged all four women to the home of a powerful friend, pushed them to their knees, ordered another friend to "hol[d] a good cudgel over their backs," and demanded that the women confess "as ever they would passe thence a live" (sig. B2v), but they refused (Fig. 2). He eventually engaged in two spectacularly unsuccessful experiments in proof through thatch burning involving a pound of melted brimstone, a quarter pound of gun powder, a giant piece of dry linen, a match at the end of a long stick, and a flaming arrow, all of which ill-fatedly failed to ignite the thatch (sig. D1r).

2.2 (Mis)Trusting the Senses: Skeptics, the Devil's Juggling, and Other Theatrical Illusions

Many demonologists and accusers similarly frustrated in their attempts to extirpate the "wéedes" of witchcraft viewed skepticism as the culprit. Prominent skeptics like Johann Weyer or Reginald Scot, they argued, made justices doubt even the clearest evidence. Scholars sometimes claim that even those skeptical about the

[35] Perkins, *Discourse*, 214–15. [36] Cotta, *Triall*, 83, 28, 19. [37] Perkins, *Discourse*, 214.
[38] Galis, *Brief*, sig. A3r, C4v. The in-text citations that follow are to this text.

Figure 1 Richard Galis drags a Windsor witch to the High Sheriff's lodgings, begging him to prosecute. Galis, *A Brief Treatise Containing the Most Strange and Horrible Cruelty of Elizabeth Stile Alias Rockingham and her Confederates* (1579), sig. C3r. The Bodleian Libraries, University of Oxford, Gough Berks 1

guilt of the accused or the fairness of judicial procedures nevertheless believed in the existence of witchcraft.[39] And yet, evidence suggests that many people did in fact believe that so-called witchcraft was mere demonic delusion. Certainly, demonologists thought there were many such skeptics. Witch prosecutor and judge Pierre de Lancre (a leading figure in the Labourd witch hunt of 1609, responsible for the execution of at least seventy people) explains in his *Tableau of the Inconstancy of Evil Angels and Demons* (1612): "the difficulty of proof stems from the incredulity of the judges" – the fact that they view witchcraft as mere "fabl[e] and illusio[n]." This leads them to acquit, he complains, "fantastically multipl[ying] the number of witches who flourish everywhere today."[40] Or, as the

[39] See e.g. Levack, *Witch-Hunt*, 231.
[40] Lancre, *Tableau*, 273, 382, 271 (*On the Inconstancy*, 285, 393, 282, translation modified).

Figure 2 Richard Galis threatens four alleged witches with a cudgel to get them to confess. Galis, *A Brief Treatise Containing the Most Strange and Horrible Cruelty of Elizabeth Stile Alias Rockingham and her Confederates* (1579), sig. B1v. The Bodleian Libraries, University of Oxford, Gough Berks 1

judge declares in the 1603 case of the alleged werewolf Jean Grenier (which I discuss in Section 2.7): there are jurists who "rejec[t] as fables and illusions all that witches say of their idolatries, . . .dances, transports in the air, and transformations," granting them "impunity [and] wondrously multiply[ing] the number of witches, . . . to the ruin of Christendom."[41]

In fact, treatises championing the extermination of witches usually identify skepticism – and the urgent necessity of refuting it – as their *raison d'être*. De Lancre explains that the aim of his book is to

> dispel the error of the many who deny the principles of witchcraft, believing that it is only magic, dream, and illusion [and to] clearly show that the doubt, impunity, or leniency that our fathers and the courts of *Parlement* showed toward it until now nourished and preserved the false belief and allowed it to multiply.[42]

[41] Mandrou, *Possession*, 66–7.

[42] Lancre, *Tableau*, sig. é1v (*On the Inconstancy*, 1, translation modified).

Similarly, the French judge-prosecutor Henry Boguet, who oversaw the execution of at least forty witches in Saint-Claude, Burgundy, between 1596 and 1616, begins the preface to his influential *Discourse of Witches Drawn from Several Trials with . . . Instructions for a Judge* (1602): "It is astonishing that there should still be found today people who do not believe that there are witches."[43] The great political theorist and demonologist Jean Bodin explains that he "decided to write [his] treatise," *The Demon-Mania of Witches* (1580), because of the urgency of answering "those who in printed books try to save witches by every means." Satan himself inspires people "to publish these fine books [teaching] that there are no spirits . . . or witches," leading "judges [to] g[i]ve up their pursuit of witches," thus allowing "witches [to] multipl[y] and greatly increas[e] in number."[44] Such declarations remind us that skepticism was not merely a *reaction* to the demonological theory: it helped *produce* that theory and the witch-hunting that flowed from it. The most virulent and influential demonological treatises were attempts to refute the skeptics. These then served as guides to prosecution.[45] One might almost say that skepticism gave rise to the witch hunts.

According to the conventional narrative, it was a new belief in direct sensory experience that led to the growth of skepticism, eventually replacing the belief in authoritative texts on which the trials had been founded. But in fact believers often cited empirical evidence for witchcraft as grounds for belief. Conversely, skeptics often cited authoritative texts (especially religious ones) as grounds for disbelief.[46] It is worth recalling that such influential demonologists as Bodin, Boguet, de Lancre, or the Lorraine witch prosecutor Nicolas Rémy wrote from their firsthand experience as judges, witchcraft prosecutors, or judicial consultants, reporting what they witnessed in trials (a fact that the fantastical nature of their demonologies tends to obscure). That is, they based their texts at least in part on what they had directly "seen, heard, and tested," as Boguet explains he has done.[47] Jurists dedicated to the elimination of witchcraft often claimed that empirical evidence was at least as necessary as confession to conviction, and in some cases superior. The "strongest" and "clearest proof" ("stronger than all the testimony in the world, or even voluntary confessions"), explains Bodin, is

43 Boguet, *Discours des sorciers*, sig. A3v (*Examen*, xxxix, translation modified).

44 Bodin, *De la démonomanie*, 61 (*On the Demon-Mania*, 37–8, answering those who found a recent case over which he presided "unbelievable"). Bodin devotes a long final section of his treatise to a "Réfutation des opinions de Jean Wier" (*De la démonomanie*, 437–90).

45 For a classic discussion of this point, see Clark, *Thinking*, 195–213.

46 The terms "believers" and "skeptics" act as convenient shorthand but oversimplify, since these came in many varieties. Virtually all skeptics believed that witches had once existed (on biblical authority), and even fervent believers could be skeptical about certain phenomena (for instance, transportation to sabbats). The views of some – Pierre Le Loyer or George Gifford, for instance – are so complex that it is difficult to classify them as either.

47 Boguet, *Discours des sorciers*, sig. A6r.

evidence that "the Judge sees, . . . or touches, or perceives, or apprehends by one of the five senses."[48] As Cotta repeatedly stresses, evidence must be demonstrated not only to the "inward understanding" but to the "outward sense."[49] What one could see with one's senses was the best answer to doubt: "the proof of all the things that we saw with our own eyes," writes de Lancre,

> the evidence . . . that we saw . . . performed in our presence, . . . must confirm for even the most stubborn, stupid, blind, and bewildered people that there is [no] doubt that Witchcraft exists.[50]

Part of what made the skeptics so convincing – and thus so dangerous – was that skeptics and believers in fact began with the same premise: that the devil (that old juggler and father of lies) could create phantasms, and thus (as everyone knew) one could not trust the evidence of one's senses.[51] On the one hand, as believers argued, what appeared capable of natural explanation might in fact be witchcraft, for the devil used trickery to conceal the work of his minions. If witchcraft could appear to the senses, it could also (as de Lancre explains) "block the flow of the senses."[52] On the other hand, as skeptics argued, what appeared witchcraft might instead be diabolical delusion. Believers had to cede the point. The devil could produce "delusions, whereby mens senses are . . . corrupted," allows Perkins, "illusion[s] of the outward senses, . . . wherby he makes a man to thinke that he heareth, seeth, feeleth or toucheth such things as indeede he doth not."[53]

It was not, of course, only the devil who created illusions: people did too, as skeptics were quick to point out, most notably charlatan magicians and counterfeit demoniacs. "[F]rom the beginning of the world till this daie," declares Scot, "never [has] any [magician or witch] yet . . . shewed any other . . . cunning point of witchcraft, than legierdemaine or cousenage." As for the possessed who cry "witch," their "feats, illusions, and transes" are "a hundred cousenages," allowing poor women to be "arraigned upon . . . a false lie, devised by [a] juggler, through the malicious instigation of some of hir adversaries."[54] Believers could not deny that many of the supposedly possessed had confessed to counterfeiting. In fact,

48 Bodin, *De la démonomanie*, 366 (*On the Demon-Mania*, 181).

49 Cotta, *Triall*, 8 (and, generally, on the reliability of things "manifest to sense," 10, 13, 18, 27, 31, 38, 41, 75, 78, 82, 84, 100).

50 Lancre, *Tableau*, sig. é2r (*On the Inconstancy*, 3, translation modified). And later: "cela se voit a l'œil . . .: par ainsi [on voit que] ce n'est pas illusion" (*Tableau*, 538 [*On the Inconstancy*, 540]).

51 For examples of the commonplace that the devil is the "father of lies," see Institoris, *Malleus*, 189A (*Hammer*, 489); Gifford, *Dialogue*, sig. I1v, I2v; *Witches of Northampton-Shire*, sig. B1r.

52 Lancre, *Tableau*, 291 (*On the Inconstancy*, 305).

53 Perkins, *Discourse*, 23.

54 Scot, *Discoverie*, 482, 131, 126, 130 (Bk. 16, Ch. 6; Bk. 7, Ch. 1). Here Scot is specifically describing the case of Mildred Norrington, a seventeen-year-old demoniac who later confessed to counterfeiting, but his argument that demoniacs are counterfeiters (melancholics aside) is a more general one.

witch-hunting enthusiasts tended to condemn charlatans and counterfeiters in even stronger terms than skeptics. The counterfeit demoniac was like an actor but worse, argued the Puritan divine Richard Bernard in his *Guide to Grand-Jury Men* (1627), for "he goeth about to counterfeite, not professedly, as Stage-Players doe," but in a deliberate effort to deceive.[55] For enemies of witchcraft like Bernard, such mountebank actors undermined the true cause by creating skeptics. Defending the exorcist John Darrell (on trial for fraudulent exorcism), one pamphleteer explains that the numerous cases of counterfeiting cause "witchcraft [to be] called into question" and "Atheists [to] abound in these dayes." Given the fact that so many have counterfeited possession, why "should [people] thinke there is any possession at all?"[56]

Judges' and jurors' knowledge that many had counterfeited did in fact sometimes make them skeptical: when Mary Glover began to go into fits at the trial of Elizabeth Jackson in 1602, the judges and spectators cried out, "shee counterfetteth," "shee counterfetteth"![57] In fact, even believers acknowledged that there were counterfeiters. But as they stressed, the existence of charlatans and counterfeiters did not mean that *all* were charlatans and counterfeiters.[58] Nor did the existence of diabolical deception mean that all evidence of witchcraft was deception.[59] One simply had to distinguish the true from the false. This might be difficult. Bernard notes that "some can so lively resemble" the "distortio[n]s, perturbations, agitations, writhings, tumblings, tossings, wallowings, foamings" of the possessed that the spectators think counterfeiters bewitched merely because "they seeme [so] in outward apparance."[60] Still harder was piercing the veil of diabolical deception. "[H]ow shall wee discry the practise of devils, who are far more deepe and subtil, and can cover their sleights and false conveiances more craftily then men [?]" asks the Puritan divine George Gifford in his *Discourse of the Subtill Practises of Devilles by Witches and Sorcerers* (1587).[61]

---

[55] Bernard, *Guide*, 44. On the early modern identification of counterfeiting with theater, see Greenblatt, "Loudun" and "Shakespeare." As "jugglers" and illusion-makers, the devil, sorcerers, and witches were also, of course, identified with theater.

[56] *Triall of Maist. Dorrell*, 7. [57] Bradwell, "Mary Glovers," 22.

[58] See e.g. Bradwell's response to physician Edward Jorden's observation on Mary Glover's demonstration of possession that "*some have counterfeited possessions*": "And what then?" Bradwell, "Mary Glovers," 68.

[59] See, for instance, de Lancre: "Bien que plusieurs personnes souffrent illusion ce n'est pas à dire que tout ce que le Diable opere en nous soit illusion" (*Tableau*, 86 [*On the Inconstancy*, 111]).

[60] Bernard, *Guide*, 29.

[61] Gifford, *Discourse*, sig. B1r. Scholars often treat Gifford as an opponent of witchcraft prosecutions and a skeptic because he vigorously protested that neighborhood quarrels, ignorance, and the devil's mischief created false accusations and resulted in the execution of the innocent. But in both of his works on witchcraft, he repeatedly stresses that "For the rooting out of witches, the Scripture is plaine. *Thou shalt not suffer a witch to live*" (*Dialogue*, sig. D1r).

Gifford's answer is similar to Augustine's answer to skeptics: with due caution, you *can* trust your senses.[62] In support of this view, he cites the stories of doubting Thomas and the Apostles' discovery of the resurrected Jesus, which he counterintuitively reads as parables of the superiority of visual and tactile evidence over faith. In John 20:29, Jesus allows doubting Thomas to see the imprint of the nails in his hands and feel the wound in his side, but adds: "blessed *are* they that have not seene, and [yet] have beleeved."[63] Ignoring this line, with its claim for the superiority of faith over visual evidence, Gifford argues that Thomas's problem was that he "woulde not trust his sight." Jesus's statement to Thomas (in Gifford's rendering), "thou doest believe because thou hast seene," is not descriptive but imperative: "believe because thou hast seene."[64]

Gifford was not alone in viewing the senses as the best guide in matters of witchcraft.[65] Where he calls upon biblical authority, Cotta calls upon the authority of common experience, but they come to the same conclusion: one can in fact trust "the eye and eare" and the "five senses" generally to distinguish true witchcraft from delusion. Observation tells us, explains Cotta, that "it is not a thing impossible, but usuall and familiar unto all kinde of men, ... to distinguish betweene those things which are only in imagination, and those which are reall and indeede." We do this when we look at paintings, awaken from dreams, or even watch entertainers' "juggling deceit[s]." In these, our sensory faculties guide us, allowing us to "compar[e] that which [i]s seene, with that which is not seene; that is, the counterfait with the true substance." The eye can distinguish genuine acts of witchcraft from the devil's "juggling deceit[s]" because, insists Cotta, a "juggling deceit" is always knowne ... by the eye."[66]

2.3 Evidentiary Doctrine Meets Performance Proof

The challenge was thus to make genuine acts of witchcraft *legally* visible. In the *Malleus maleficarum* (*Hammer of Witches*) (1487) – arguably the foundational text of witchcraft prosecutions – Heinrich Institoris had explained that judges, accusers, and others were permitted "to use many lawful stratagems both in words and deeds" to produce proof of witchcraft.[67] One such stratagem was the

[62] Augustine, *De civitate dei*, 685–6 (Bk. 19, Ch. 18). [63] *Bible*, fol. 489r.

[64] In the same passage, Gifford argues that Jesus uses sensory evidence to debunk the apostles' fear that he is a spirit, identifying Jesus's validation of sensory evidence ("handle" and "see") as confirmation that we can trust our senses when we believe we see spirits or witches. Gifford, *Discourse*, sig. F4r (referencing Luke 24:39–40).

[65] See, similarly, Bradwell, "Mary Glovers," 92–3 (fol. 114v) and Pierre Le Loyer's extended refutation of skeptics who doubt the evidence of the senses: it is precisely the senses that prove the existence of spirits (Le Loyer, *Discours*, 35–46 [Ch. 6]).

[66] Cotta, *Triall*, 2, 82–4.

[67] Institoris, *Malleus*, 228B (*Hammer*, 585). See similarly Rémy, *Daemonolatreiae*, 357 (Bk. 3, Ch. 9; *Demonolatry*, 168).

staging of the kinds of scenes that I describe at the beginning of this Element. Confuting skepticism, such staging could provide proof that the spectators could "se[e], … or touc[h], or perceiv[e], or kno[w] by means of one of the five senses."[68] Such evidence answered the skeptics not verbally but in the form of "acts of Sorcery and Witch-craft manifest to sense." When, for instance, a disbeliever came to view the thirteen-year-old demoniac Thomas Darling in 1596 and told the boy that "there was no witches" and he "should not dissemble," Darling responded by instantly going into a "cruell fit."[69]

Reductively, such performance proof was of three basic (though often overlapping) types: performance of seemingly actual witchcraft; experimental demonstration that the accused had power over victims and that they were not counterfeiting; and the staging of a sudden revelation that seemed instantly dispositive. As I note in the Introduction, three important evidentiary doctrines, which appear in both Roman-canon and English common law variants, are especially illuminating for understanding these three kinds of scenes: "taking [the criminal] in the acte" ("*in flagrante*"); establishing the "*notorious evidence of the facte*" (or "*notoriety of the fact*"); and producing "violent presumptions" (or "*indicia indubitata*") of guilt.[70] All three were (according to English jurist Richard Cosin) "*sundry meanes*" of "finding out of *Trueth*" when, as in most witchcraft accusations, ordinary methods "doe want." For both English and continental jurists, any of the three constituted "full proofe": grounds not just for investigation but for conviction.[71] Judges often cited these doctrines. But they could also appear in informal evidentiary language or in attempts to catch the accused in the act, show that her guilt was notorious, or create a scene that would appear dispositive.

Surprisingly, it was not merely accusers or judges and prosecutors who staged such "sure proofe." It was often the accused themselves: those who had confessed but sought to further persuade judges and audiences of the truth of their confessions. Scholars have considered the variety of reasons the accused often confessed: because they were subject to torture (or threatened with torture); because harsh prison conditions could amount to torture;

[68] Bodin, *De la démonomanie*, 366 (*On the Demon-Mania*, 181).

[69] *Most Wonderfull and True Storie*, 15–16.

[70] Cosin, *Apologie*, Part 2: 64, 73, 10, 63 (parts separately paginated: hereafter cited in the text with part number followed by page number). Such Roman-canon evidentiary doctrines were already present in Bracton in the thirteenth century, and later English jurists (demonologists in particular) drew extensively on continental jurists' discussions of "presumptions," "circumstances," "full proof," and more (see Shapiro, "*Beyond*," especially 51–4, 164–8). Cosin's treatise is technically about ecclesiastical law and not specifically about witchcraft, but Cosin is useful here both because he routinely identifies the English common law equivalents of Roman-canon law doctrines and because he offers a particularly clear exposition of these doctrines.

[71] Cosin, *Apologie*, 2:52, 2:62–3.

because they were despairing and suicidal; because they were promised mercy if they confessed; because they believed that they were witches or in fact practiced magic; because threatening to perform witchcraft offered emotional release (and sometimes got results); or because the celebrity confession promised was too tempting to resist.[72] Where judges or juries were skeptical about confessions, performance could convince them to believe.

2.4 Taking the Witch "in the Acte": Performing the Crime Itself in the Courtroom

In 1590, the twenty-four-year-old King James VI of Scotland (later, James I of England) called several accused witches to Holyroodhouse, the royal residence in Edinburgh, and proceeded to conduct pretrial examinations in his chamber. The scenes that took place during these examinations were described in a lurid pamphlet, *News from Scotland*, published soon after the events, probably written by James Carmichael, Minister of Haddington.[73] Among those James examined was Geillis Duncan, a young servant who had allegedly led the dance at a witches' sabbat at North Berwick Kirk, playing "upon a small Trump" (a Jew's harp), while everyone danced and sang a witches' song ("*Cammer* [friend] *go ye before, commer go ye*; / *If ye will not go before, commer let me*"). In James's chamber (according to the *News*), Geillis proceeded "upon the like trump [to play] the said dance before the king's Majesty" (315). Soon after, a healer, diviner, and midwife named Agnes Sampson offered a display of clairvoyance, in which she was able to tell James "the very words which passed between the king's Majesty and his queen . . . the first night of their marriage" (316). Soon after that, James examined Doctor John Fian (alias Cunningham), a schoolmaster and town lothario who had supposedly confessed to putting a hex on a love rival that drove the man mad. Fian "caused the gentleman to be brought before the king's Majesty" to display his "lunacy": the man "gave a great screech" and "fell into a madness, sometime bending himself, and sometime capering so directly up, that his head did touch the ceiling of the chamber" (318–19).

According to the pamphlet, James was initially skeptical. The confessions were "so miraculous and strange as that his Majesty said they were all extreme liars" (316). In the pamphlet's rendering, the aim of the performances was to overcome James's skepticism: Fian declared that he was bringing the bewitched

[72] For a discussion of confession as a form of female self-fashioning, see Purkiss, *Witch*, 145–76.

[73] The title on the 1591 pamphlet appears as *Newes from Scotland*. I have followed the text in Normand and Roberts, *Witchcraft*. The in-text citations that follow are to this text. On "cammer" or "commer," see Normand and Roberts, *Witchcraft*, 326.

man "for the verity of the same" (318); Sampson declared that "she would not wish his Majesty to suppose her words to be false, but rather to believe them," promising proof that "his Majesty should not any way doubt of." After a display of her powers, James "swore by the living God that he believed that all the devils in hell could not have discovered the same" (316). The accused, through their performances, had made him a believer.

These scenes speak, at a minimum, to the *desire* for evidentiary performance that could answer James's skepticism. But there is in fact reason to believe that some version of what the *News* reports took place, however sensationalist the account. James was present at the examinations, and Carmichael was close to the king, in Edinburgh at the time, and almost certainly an eyewitness.[74] Fian, Duncan, and Sampson had a strong motive for demonstrating the sincerity of their confessions: they had been repeatedly tortured, and continued to confess (with a certain urgency) until just before their executions.[75] The pamphlet is dominated by fantastical stories of witchcraft: a christened cat that conjures a raging tempest in the North Sea; a scene in which Fian bewitches the hair of a young virgin heifer, which pursues him into his church mooing amorously; a sabbat in which the devil commands that all the witches "kiss his buttocks in sign of duty to him; which being put over the pulpit bare, everyone did as he had enjoined them" (317, 320, 315). By contrast, the scenes in the examination chamber are within the realm of the more than possible: a tune on a Jew's harp with a dance; a performance of madness with some high leaps; and a wedding-night secret discovered by a woman who turns out to be an "old acquaintance" of the servant in charge of the king's bedchamber (316). While almost pitifully prosaic, these performances produced "wonder" and "admiration" (316): their ability to realize witchcraft in the examination room made them *appear* astonishing enough to stand as proof.

One critic has suggested that there was no such thing as entirely direct, unmediated evidence in the early modern courtroom, for "criminal actio[n] can't ever be literally reproduced in court."[76] But the performances of witchcraft for James (and others we will encounter) were not merely *representations* of the crime, but the crime *itself*, performed before the very eyes of the royal judge. Cosin identifies this kind of evidence in its Greek-biblical, Roman, and English versions. It is

[74] See Normand and Roberts, *Witchcraft*, 128.

[75] Their confessions appear in the examinations and "dittays" (indictments) in Normand and Roberts, *Witchcraft*, 135–57, 164–7, 174, 205–11, 224–46.

[76] Mukherji, "Knowing Encounters."

> that detection which the *Grecians* call ἐπ' αὐτοφόρῳ [in the act]. So was the woman taken in the very acte of adulterie in the *Gospel*. The *Latines* terme it thus; *Deprehensio in flagranti crimine* [discovery in flagrant crime]. And upon the borders of *England*, taking one *with the bloodie hand*; or (as it is more commonly expressed) taking an offendour *with the manner*.[77]

Being taken "in the very acte" is grounds not merely for suspicion but for conviction. Cosin imagines the ideal witness to such evidence to be not an ordinary person but (like James) "a Judge himselfe (sitting publikely) [who himself] seeth some crime committed" (2:64). In such a case, the judge need not trust the narration of a witness-middleman: he sees it with his own eyes. The judge is simultaneously judge and witness, a witness "aswell as any cōmon person there, that might happen to have heard it or seene it" (2:89). In fact, in common law courts there are many such moments, says Cosin: for example, "a Cut-purse [is] espied" mid-pickpocket "by the Judge himselfe sitting on the bench," and the judge "cause[s] [him] to be staied, . . . *endited* upon [the judge's] relation" (his eyewitness testimony), and "presently tried and condemned" (2:89).

James was not the only legal authority to produce in-court witchcraft as *in flagrante* evidence. In fact, demonologists had long recommended production of the crime as a mode of proof. In the *Malleus maleficarum*, for instance – instructing the reader in how an accused witch could be tricked into performing magic before an official – Institoris had described a recent case. The governor of Königsheim Castle in Saxony pretended that he was away but commandeered three of the accused's friends to promise her freedom if she would demonstrate her craft. Eventually she acquiesced: "a dish full of water was brought to her, [and] the sorceress told [the one who brought it] to set the water in motion a little with a finger." She uttered certain words and suddenly there was a "greater downpour of hail than had been seen for many years."[78] Bodin describes a case in which a judicial official forced a witch to cure her victim with witchcraft. She "invoked the Devil, muttering several charms with her face to the earth in everyone's presence." She then "gave [a small] packet to the [bewitched]," which contained three live lizards, and told him that "he should put what was in the packet in his bath while saying the words, '*Va de par le Diable*.'" According to Bodin, he did this and was cured.[79] In his *Investigations into Magic* (1599–1600), the Jesuit demonologist Martín Del Río describes an inquisitor in Pompey who ordered a sorcerer to fly if he could: "[s]traight away, the man was lifted up into

[77] Cosin, *Apologie*, 2:64. ἐπ' αὐτοφόρῳ is Cosin's rendering of επαυτοφωρω (from John 8:4). See, similarly, Sir Thomas Smith: a criminal may be "taken with the maner, which in Latine they call *inflagranti crimine*" (*De Republica Anglorum*, 78; and, similarly, Smith, *Common-welth*, 101).

[78] Institoris, *Malleus*, 217C–D (*Hammer*, 559).

[79] Bodin, *De la démonomanie*, 329.

the air."[80] Some such accounts are clearly fabrications or phantasms. But many of them are feasible enough to be credible, and some seem merely slightly exaggerated by the perceptions of spectators eager to see a chance rainstorm as a diabolical hailstorm or a balletic leap as a sorcerer in flight.

Faced with the demand that they perform witchcraft for the judge, some of the accused declared their innocence and thus their inability to do so. But many did what they could. It was not hard to perform a witch's dance or act a mad scene. One could easily imitate demoniacs to suggest that one was both possessed and a witch, as Rollande du Vernois did for Boguet (in a case that I will discuss further in Section 3.1). But where judges demanded that the accused reproduce some of the more extraordinary feats to which they had confessed, we often find them offering excuses. At the first Chelmsford witch trial in 1566, Queen's Attorney Sir Gilbert Gerard demanded that Mother Waterhouse summon her familiar – "a thynge lyke a blacke dogge with [a] face like an ape a short taile . . . and a peyre of hornes on his heade" – to "come before us nowe," promising: "if ye can[,] we will dyspatche you out of pryson by and by." She apologized, explaining: "no faith, . . . I can not, for in faith if I had let hym go as my daughter did I could make hym come by and by, but now I have no more power over him."[81] Boguet describes an examination of several people accused of lycanthropy (becoming wolves to perform *maleficium*). When he demands that they turn themselves into wolves right then and there, they explain to him that unfortunately "it was impossible for them to turn themselves into wolves, since they had no more ointment, and they had lost the power of doing so by being imprisoned."[82]

If "the Judge himselfe sitting on the bench" witnessed the witch *in flagrante*, surely this was proof that would convince even the skeptics. While the lycanthropists were momentarily unable to turn themselves into wolves, Boguet has (he writes) "*seen* [them] go on all-fours in a room just as they did when they were in the fields," and asks: "Who now can doubt but that these witches themselves . . . committed the acts and murders?"[83] How could James doubt after he had seen the witches themselves perform their witchcraft? The spectator's wonder underlined the supernatural nature of the performance and thus its authenticity: this could be no counterfeiting, for such things were impossible without witchcraft. Wonder led not to doubt but to belief.

80 Del Río, *Disquisitiones*, 60 (Bk. 5, Sec. 7; *Investigations*, 214).

81 Phillips, *Examination*, sig. A4v, A7r–v.

82 Boguet, *Discours des sorciers*, 121 (*Examen*, 151). Boguet believes that such transformations are not actually possible: Satan gives witches the illusion that they have become wolves, allowing them to go into the fields and commit murder (*Discours*, 118).

83 Boguet, *Discours des sorciers*, 121–2 (*Examen*, 151).

2.5 Performing Judicial Countermagic

If it was uncommon for judges to demand that the accused bring on a hailstorm or turn themselves into wolves, the demand that they perform countermagic was in fact fairly standard. As in the cases of Françoise Fontaine and John Samuel (which I discuss in Sections 3 and 4), the judge would often, for instance, order the accused to recite a charm or spell conjuring the devil and commanding him to stop tormenting the bewitched. In a typical case in the Parlement of Paris in 1583, the judge ordered an alleged sorcerer to say the words: "Devil, I conjure you and I take you for mine; . . . [l]eave the body of this child and never enter it again."[84] The spell was to serve two functions simultaneously: the evidentiary function of displaying the power of the accused to stop the bewitched victim's fits; and the curative, countermagic function of eradicating the harm (eventually completed through the execution of the witch). *News from Scotland* enthusiastically describes the court's employment of several accused witches to get John Fian to confess, which they did by removing "charmed pins" from under his tongue and chanting "'Now is the charm stinted.'"[85] De Lancre describes the somewhat more dramatic case of judges who, in the midst of a witch trial, decide to attend a witches' sabbat themselves, presumably to gather evidence (but also, as de Lancre explains, "goaded by some pernicious curiosity"). The devil "really transports [such] judges bodily through the air . . . to the sabbat," explains de Lancre, but he leaves a witch behind – "not [her] real body, but her form and image" – in order to trick the judges into "believ[ing] the[ir] transport to the sabbath to be [only] an illusion, . . . thereby blocking the execution of justice."[86]

Bringing witchcraft or the devil into the courtroom raised two related concerns. First, even if one was producing countermagic, was it permissible? Sixteenth-century demonologists sometimes reiterated Institoris's recommendations that judges prepare themselves to "assai[l] [the witch] in manly fashion" by bringing her into the courtroom backwards (to prevent her from mesmerizing them with her eyes). Before the trial, judges were to protect themselves by eating exorcised salt, carrying a blessed palm, hanging the seven words Christ uttered on the cross around the witch's neck, and binding a piece of "Blessed Wax the length of Christ's body . . . to her naked body." Institoris reassures readers that canon law permits such countermagic to "brea[k] and hinde[r] greater acts of sorcery."[87] But demonologists often forbade such strategies. "Let us not ourselves dabble in those arts which we condemn," writes Rémy in his *Daemonolatreiae* (1595), and

[84] Jacques-Chaquin and Préaud, *Sorciers*, 259. [85] Normand and Roberts, *Witchcraft*, 318.

[86] Lancre, *Tableau*, 86 (*On the Inconstancy*, 112, translation modified). De Lancre critiques this "damnable curiosity," but perhaps – spending his days steeped in demonology – he in fact dreamed of sabbats and believed he had attended them.

[87] Institoris, *Malleus*, 216B, 214C (*Hammer*, 556, 552).

"aggravate the offence by committing it under the cloak of law and justice."[88] When people who use countermagic "ascribe power unto such things to drive out devils, what are they but Witches?" asks Gifford. "O wretched men so relieved: they do imagine that the devill is driven out of them [but] he hath entred in déeper. For can that which is devilish, as a charme, drive out the devil?"[89] As Bodin notes, "by [such] means the Devil makes Witchcraft out of Law, which ought to be sacred."[90]

Second, was it safe to bring the devil into the courtroom? When James invited the North Berwick witches into his chamber, some thought that he should "not hazard himself in the presence of such notorious witches lest thereby might have ensued great danger to his person and the general state of the land," *News from Scotland* reports. However, the king was God's particular "annointed" and the witches only weak "vessels of God's wrath," explains the pamphlet. Therefore, James was "not feared with their enchantments."[91] In his *Daemonologie* (1597), James himself makes the classic more general argument that God protects anyone acting in the name of the law: "For where God beginnes justlie to strike by his lawful Lieutennentes, it is not in the Devilles power to defraude or bereave him of the office, or effect of his powerfull and revenging Scepter."[92]

Some disagreed. In a chapter that Boguet added to the 1606 edition of his *Discourse of Witches*, titled "That Satan companies with his Witches when they are in Prison and even Assists them in the Presence of the Judge," he asks: "But what stronger confirmation . . . could we wish than that which happens when the Judge examines witches? For at that time the Devil assists them and advises them what to answer."[93] In either case, in the courtroom the judge was on the front lines of the battle against the devil. The only way to win that battle was to summon the devil to the courtroom and confront him. One's only choice might be to use one kind of witchcraft to defy the other.

2.6 Establishing the "Notoriety of the Fact" through "Open Triall"

On October 18th, 1602, John Croke, judge and Recorder of London (the city's chief legal officer), brought fourteen-year-old Mary Glover and Elizabeth Jackson – an elderly charwoman whom Mary had accused of witchcraft – to his chambers in the Inner Temple. According to physician Stephen Bradwell's

88 Rémy, *Daemonolatreiae*, 361 (Bk. 3, Ch. 9; *Demonolatry*, 170). See a similar critique of Institoris in Boguet, *Discours des sorciers*, 170.

89 Gifford, *Discourse*, sig. H3r, H1v. 90 Bodin, *De la démonomanie*, 402.

91 Normand and Roberts, *Witchcraft*, 323–4.

92 *Daemonologie*, 51. See, similarly, Fulbeck, *Parallele*, fol. 98v.

93 Boguet, *Discours execrable*, 251, 255 (*Examen*, 132, 134–5).

detailed account of the case, Mary's family had already engaged in various public experiments aimed at demonstrating the truth of Mary's accusation: before her uncle Sir William Glover (Alderman and Sheriff of London); Sir John Harte (a former Lord Mayor); Lady Bruckard; "many divines"; and others.[94] Croke himself had already tried his own experiments to test Jackson's guilt. In his chambers, he planned to produce the fourth such "experiment" to definitively "fin[d] out of trueth" before "many witnesses" (20–2). For this one, Croke did something novel. Having selected a woman "very comparable" to Jackson to impersonate her ("aged, homely, grosse bodyed, and of lowe stature"), he dressed her in Jackson's hat and wrapped a muffler round her face, so that "muffled and disguised, . . . there was no dissimilitude in the outward forme of the person, [and] [i]t was very easie for the maide to thinke it was that verie woman" (21, 65–6). Leading the disguised woman into the chamber where Mary was waiting, he "caused [Mary] to touch the woman diverse times, using words [that] implyed, it was [Jackson]; saying he hoped [Mary] should thereafter, never more have cause to be affrayde of her" (65). When Mary did not react, he led the woman out and brought in Jackson herself, "having on the other womans hat, with a Cloak and muffler; so as none could know who she was" (21). As he brought the two toward each other, Mary fell into a fit, becoming a "senseles image throwen upon a bed" with a demonic "voyce in her nostrills," which said: "hang her" (21, 23). Now mostly persuaded of Jackson's guilt, Croke dismissed the long line of "new maskers [waiting] to enter" (21).

The final experiments took place in the courtroom itself during the trial before the judge (Sir Edmund Anderson), the jury, and numerous witnesses and general spectators. Attempting to test whether Mary could sense Jackson's presence without seeing her, they placed Mary "with her face towards the bench" (22). According to Bradwell's report,

> at the judgment seat, when this maid stood forth to geve in her evidence, not seeing the woman (who stood in the dock a pretye distaunce of, and manie persons betweene) yet . . . she cryed, where is shee? '*Where is she that troubleth me*' and so fell downe. (66)

Then "her body [writhed] so far over to the left side" that her right hip bone was "where the lefte should stand" (22–3), and she uttered in that same demonic voice, "*hang her*" (22–3). This performance did not persuade everyone. As people cried out, "shee counterfetteth," several men carried her into an adjoining chamber. Anderson, Croke, the town clerk, various officers, "and divers other Justices" followed soon after (22–3). According to Bradwell, they entered "with thundring

[94] For details, see the introduction in MacDonald, *Witchcraft* (and xiv on the position of Recorder of London). In-text citations here are to Bradwell, "Mary Glovers."

voyces crying; bring the fyre, and hot Irons, for this Counterfett; Come wee will marke her, on the Cheeke, for a Counterfett" (23), a melodramatic rendering of what was probably a more dispassionate attempt to reproduce some of Croke's earlier tests for counterfeiting. Examining Mary's strange posture and the stiffness of her body, "Mr Recorder againe with a fyred paper burnt her hand, untill it blistered," but she remained impassive (23). When officers brought Jackson into the chamber, Mary again cried "*Hange her*" in her demonic voice (so audibly that those in the courtroom could hear her) and, when she felt Jackson's hand, "the maides body . . . was presently throwen, and casted with great vyolence" (23–4). Jackson's guilt was already a "notorious fact." But its demonstration through "the greivous affliction of the maide even in presence of Courte," declared John Swan, proved it even to those who ask "whether there be any witches": "the Jurie hath found it, and the Honorable Judges determined so of it."[95]

The doctrine holding that "notorious evidence of the fact" or "notoriety of the fact" ("*notorietas facti*") serves as grounds for conviction without further evidence appears in both Roman-canon and English common law. For instance, a statute in the first year of Elizabeth's reign specifies that either a "verdict of twelve men, or . . . confession, or . . . the notorious evidence of the facte" is sufficient for conviction: no jury needed.[96] A "notorious fact" (writes John Colleton in a classic formulation) "so exhibiteth it selfe to the eye . . . of all men, as that it can not be hid or excused by any colour, or tergiversation [evasion] soever."[97] Jurists commonly contrasted the *notorietas facti* not only with notoriety of law (things already judicially ascertained) but with mere rumor.[98] "Notorious defamation" only "yeeldeth a strong suspition" (explains Perkins [201]). But the "notorious fact" requires no further proof: For why (asks Cosin) "shoulde a Judge require" more "where the crime is notoriously and plainely committed?"[99] The rhetoric defining "notoriety of the fact" stresses materialized action (*factum* is a thing done, a deed), visibility, and collective spectatorship. The notorious fact is "manifest" or e-*vid*-ent in the etymological sense (known "from seeing"); it "exhibiteth it selfe to the eye . . . of all men"; it "can not be dissembled," writes Colleton, for its "witnes is the people."[100]

95 Swan, *True and Breife Report*, 3–4, 59.

96 *Anno primo Reginae Elizabethae*, sig. B2v (and see Cosin 2:73).

97 Colleton, *Just Defence*, 233 (and, similarly, 181, 213). See also Cosin, *Apologie*, 2:64; Blackwell, *Large Examination*, 43–4.

98 For a discussion of the degrees of fame that trigger a likely presumption of guilt and may add up to a full proof, see Cosin 2:56–8. Boguet argues that the "*bruit commun*" does not normally produce even light presumptions, but in cases of a "*crime excepté*" such as witchcraft, "*bruit commun*" along with other indices allows one to proceed to torture (*Discours des sorciers*, 177).

99 Cosin 2:64. See also Cosin 2:122 on "*notoriousnesse* of the fact" or "*notorious evidence* of the fact."

100 Colleton, *Just Defence*, 233–4.

Some facts became notorious all on their own. In the story of Tamar, explains Cosin, Tamar's visible pregnancy offered "*notorious evidence* of the fact" of her adultery, justifying Judah in sentencing her to "be burned."[101] (Cosin does not mention the story's central irony: that it is Judah himself who has gotten her pregnant.) Other facts needed help to become notorious, most notably hidden crimes like witchcraft. How was one to establish the notoriety of the fact of witchcraft so that it "exhibiteth it selfe to the eye . . . of all men, as that it can not be hid or excused"? Showing the witch *in flagrante* before spectators was, of course, one way of doing so. However, the accused did not always oblige by performing the crime before the judge. One might need to deploy other kinds of actors – victims like Mary Glover, for instance – who could establish the notoriety of the fact by displaying witchcraft at work on their bodies.

The now-familiar scenes of possession in the service of witchcraft accusations – public spectacles both in England and on the Continent – constituted the most common form of such efforts to establish the "notoriety of the fact." Establishing the notoriety of the fact often took the form of a quasi-scientific public experiment whose aim was to prove three separate elements: the *agent* used the *means* to cause the *harm*.[102] If taking the witch "in the acte" was a form of direct evidence, the "notorious fact" was circumstantial evidence because it required viewers to draw conclusions from inferences. (In this it was a form of "artificial proof," which, as Subha Mukherji has shown, early moderns often treated as inferior to "inartificial proofs," flipping the traditional Aristotelian hierarchy on its head.)[103] Judge Anderson admitted that Mary Glover's courtroom fit offered only circumstantial evidence, but stressed that this might be the only kind available in witchcraft cases: "you shall hardly finde any direct proofes in such a case, but by many presumptions and Circumstances, you may gather it."[104] But the distinction between direct and circumstantial evidence was not always clear, and early modern spectators often viewed such demonstrations as "direct proofes" sufficient for conviction without further evidence.

Demonstration of such proof required an "open triall" in the form of a public experiment or test.[105] Sometimes these took place in courtrooms or examination chambers, where notoriety of the fact could (as Cosin writes) "*be made to*

101 Cosin, *Apologie*, 2:122.

102 On experiments with witches both in England and on the Continent, see Stephens, *Demon Lovers*, 145–79.

103 Mukherji, *Law and Representation*, 45–7, 162–4 (and private correspondence).

104 Bradwell, "Mary Glovers," 28. See, similarly, Cotta, *Triall*, 18 (in cases of witchcraft, often "onely likelihood and presumptions doe arise in judgement" [18]); and Dalton, *Countrey Justice*, 243 ("Now against these witches the Justices of peace may not alwaies expect direct evidence").

105 For "open triall," see *Most Wonderfull and True Storie*, 14.

appeare judicially in Actes unto the Judge."[106] Often, the judge himself ordered such displays: during the trial of Anne Kereke in 1599, Anderson demanded that an allegedly bewitched girl "shew [the court] how she was tormented."[107] But one could demonstrate "*notorietie of the fact* ... in [any] great assembly of people," before spectators who could later serve as legal eyewitnesses.[108] Accusers often pointed out that such pre- or proto-evidentiary gatherings had specifically legal purposes. Hearing of the bewitching of Edward Fairfax's children, one curious traveler visited the Fairfax home with a constable and one of the accused witches and asked Fairfax permission "to satisfy himself of the truth by making such trial as he and some other strangers who came with him thought fit." Fairfax explains that he agreed because the man "used to serve upon juries at the assizes, being a freeholder of good estate, and therefore might perhaps be one upon her trial."[109]

Such public experiments might seem to herald the burgeoning culture of scientific experimentation. However, while accusers sometimes invited doctors of medicine to participate in them, they more often invited religious officials, whose experiments consisted in exorcisms or other spiritual demonstrations, or "cunning folk," whose experiments relied on folk beliefs: scratching the witch or burning her thatch or hair. Thomas Darling's family, for instance, brought a "Cunning man" and the accused witch, Alice Gooderidge, before "manie worshipful Personages ... readie to see proofe of his skill."[110] (The cunning man unfortunately turned out to be a disappointment.)

These experiments could be both curative and evidentiary. But there were others that were purely evidentiary. The most infamous (and disputed) of these was "swimming the witch." An accused witch was thrown into water: if she sank, she was innocent; if she floated, she was guilty.[111] Many – both in England and on the Continent – disapproved of "swimming," which was mostly performed at the margins of official legal proceedings. But many others would have agreed with the pamphleteer who declared swimming "an experiment that ... never failes."[112]

---

106 Cosin, *Apologie*, 2:65.

107 The pamphleteer speculates that the judge was in fact attempting "to trie ... if [sh]ee counterfeited" and was satisfied when the girl responded that "she could not shew it, but when the fit was on her." *Triall of Maist. Dorrell*, 100.

108 Cosin, *Apologie*, 2:49.

109 Fairfax, *Dæmonologia*, 80. It was, in fact, quite common to invite Justices of the Peace to witness a bewitched person's fits. See e.g. *Most Wonderfull and True Storie*, 7–8.

110 *Most Wonderfull and True Storie*, 24.

111 See James, *Daemonologie*, 81, for the theory behind swimming (the waters of baptism rejected the witch). On the test's use on the Continent, see Pihlajamäki, "'Swimming.'" On its use in England, see Darr, *Marks*, 157–71.

112 *Witches of Northampton-Shire*, sig. C2r.

Sometimes participants genuinely sought to discover the facts through such experiments. More often, however, they used them to produce legal evidence that could withstand skepticism. Such attempts were not always successful. In a well-known case, a man named Brian Gunter forced his twenty-year-old daughter Anne to feign possession, feeding her a mixture of sack and oil along with a vicious "green water" to produce vomiting and fits, in an attempt to give credibility to his witchcraft accusations.[113] He staged countless public experiments, seeking to demonstrate to skeptics that she was not counterfeiting and that his principal target, Elizabeth Gregory, was not merely "a notorious scolding body" but a notorious witch (48). At the Abingdon assizes in 1605, the judges reluctantly agreed to let him repeat his demonstrations for the jury. He carried Anne into the courtroom, and she rolled her eyes into her head on cue ("so as no part of them but the whites could be seen"), beat her knuckles against the chair (to demonstrate insensibility to pain), and finally went into a trance, falling at the feet of the jury foreman and court clerk (133). To clinch matters, Gunter demanded that Gregory recite a spell, commanding the devil to release Anne from her torments. The judges reluctantly complied, Gregory duly recited the spell, but Anne – probably exhausted and intimidated – did not react. The skeptical judge sniped: "What say you now Gunter to it [?] you have your request." Desperate for another try, Gunter protested: "She saith it not right [!]" (134). The jury's verdict: not guilty (xii, 137).

When displaying possession, accusers worked hard to refute charges that either illness or counterfeiting were responsible. During the trial of the witches of Marlou in the Loire valley in 1583, as the twelve- or thirteen-year-old demoniac Bernard Girault uttered "horrible and terrifying cries" and writhed in "astonishing torment," his parents insisted that it was obvious that their son's "torments proceed neither from nature nor coaching."[114] Bodin describes a case in which several theologians tested the veracity of a woman's claim that she was bewitched. A skeptical doctor insisted that she was merely ill with "melancholia," but after "having seen the mystery before [his] eyes, with an infinitude of people," explains Bodin, the doctor "confessed that there was an evil spirit": "[a]ll the Atheists, who deny that there are any devils," he declares, "remain mute" before such sights.[115] As *The Most Wonderfull and True Storie, of a Certaine Witch named Alse Gooderige* (1597) declared, such scenes "cr[y] out against th[e] follie" of the skeptics.[116] Experiments proved to skeptics both

[113] On the Gunter case generally, see Sharpe, *Bewitching* (and 9–10, 161, 163 on green water and sack and oil). The in-text citations that follow are to Sharpe, *Bewitching* (which quotes the original manuscript sources).

[114] Jacques-Chaquin and Préaud, *Sorciers*, 264, 266 (and 289 for Bernard's age).

[115] Bodin, *De la démonomanie*, 214–15.

[116] *Most Wonderfull and True Storie*, sig. A2v.

the fact of the witch's guilt and the existence of witches generally. "I thinke there can scarcely be any instance shewed . . . whereby . . . the peevish opinion, that there are no wiches, . . . may be better controlled than by this," exclaims *The Most Wonderfull and True Storie*. The public and notorious nature of the demonstration gave it legal ballast. If "the trueth of it . . . should be called in question," writes the pamphleteer, "a hundred more witnesses might be produced, than are here inserted."[117] As Cotta would later assert (describing "a Divell or Spirit" that appeared before the whole French court), "There could be no deceit in so many eares and witnesses."[118]

2.7 Staging Scenes to Produce "Violent Presumptions" or *Indicia Indubitata*

In 1603, a thirteen- or fourteen-year-old runaway named Jean Grenier confessed: he had the power to turn himself into a wolf, thanks to witchcraft, a pot of grease, and a wolf's skin, which "Monsieur de la Forest" (a mysterious figure with a suspicious resemblance to the devil) had given him.[119] With his father and a man called "Pierre le Tillaire," he had been running under the moon in the form of a wolf, killing and eating small children.[120] Several children had in fact recently been wounded in animal attacks or disappeared altogether. Since Jean's confession was voluntary, he repeated it *ad nauseum*, and he had a telltale witch's mark (duly pricked and found insensible) (51, 59), there was every reason to find him guilty. But the judges had their doubts (60). Jean's confession did not fit all the facts about the missing and wounded children. Each time he told his story, the details changed (52, 59). He retracted his accusations, and then reiterated them: the other werewolf was actually not Le Tillaire but a dead guy named Vincent (53); on second thought, it *was* actually Le Tillaire (57). And even if Jean were more credible (the judges wondered), did such things really happen? Many judges remained "incredul-[ous] about such things" (explains the trial report), viewing them merely as "dream[s], [or] fables and tales" (60).

But Jean was determined to prove his claims. Promising to offer irrefutable material proof in the form of the wolf's skin and pot of grease, he headed up

117 *Most Wonderfull and True Storie*, sig. A2r–v. 118 Cotta, *Triall*, 29.

119 A transcription of the trial record can be found in Mandrou, *Possession*, 33–109. The in-text citations that follow are to this text. De Lancre dedicates a long section of the *Tableau* to his own account of the case, which he bases on an interview he had with Jean some years later (*Tableau*, 254–311 [*On the Inconstancy*, 267–326]). And see Machielsen, "Making of a Teen Wolf" (analyzing the sources and de Lancre's "mental world").

120 The text variously gives the man's name as "Pierre Dechez dit Tillaire," "Pierre le Tillaire," "Pierre dit Le Tillaire," "Pierre du Tillaire qui dit s'appeler Pierre Grand," and "Pierre Grand dict de Tillaire" (53).

a judicial search party. The judges ransacked one neighbor's house after another, but no one could find the telltale items. Nothing daunted, Jean said that if they would follow him to the scene of his crimes, he could *demonstrate* his deeds *in situ* and, in so doing, offer proof that would clear all doubt. And so, leading the way, he marched off with a train of judges, prosecutors, and court officers behind him, tramping through pastures, valleys, livestock pens, under hedges and over high walls into ruined vineyards, the train growing longer as curious spectators joined (54–7). At each stop, Jean attempted to conjure up the gruesome sights and sounds of the werewolf and his prey. Here was the "broken up hedge . . . between the field and the road" where he had dragged one young girl to the "small sapwood near [the] pear tree: here were the indentations" (55). Here was the "opening in the vines through which he carried [another] first to the stone wall" (here), and then to "the old oak" (here): this was "where he removed her dress without tearing it" (as no animal could have done) "and ate her" (56). Faced with a lineup of three or four girls dressed alike and of equal height, one of whom he had allegedly attacked (an attempt to test his confession), instead of merely pointing, "he suddenly seized [one] girl" (a gasp of horror from the crowd). He then proudly displayed "the wounds he had made . . . on her chin, jaw, throat, [and] the back of her head, . . . both by teeth as well as nails" (55). This was not, of course, the crime *itself*, for Jean had not actually become a werewolf then and there. Nor was it a logical demonstration producing a *notorietas facti*. Instead, Jean performed actions that stood as *signs* of the crime: signs whose persuasive power arose in part from the shock and horror that their sudden violence produced. It worked. The judges condemned Jean to hang and his body to be burned (though the appeals court was merciful and sent him to a monastery for life) (58, 109).

According to the classic Roman law tripartite scheme, circumstantial evidence or "*indicia*" (often translated as "tokens," "marks," or "signe[s]") were of three kinds, producing "light" (*temeraria*), "probable" (*probabilis*), or "violent" (*violenta*) presumptions, sometimes known as "vehement" or "pregnant" presumptions or *indicia indubitata*.[121] The classic example of a situation producing a violent presumption was taking the criminal "with the bloodie hand" or "with the manner." Some (such as Cosin) conflated this with being taken in the act, but "the bloodie hand" was not the act itself but a sign of the act. As Bracton *On the Laws and Customs of England* had explained: when someone "is arrested over the body of the dead man with his knife dripping blood," a "violent

[121] See, for instance, Cosin, *Apologie*, 2:62, 2:92. For the application of the scheme to cases of witchcraft, see Institoris, *Malleus*, 207C, 221A–226A (*Hammer*, 535, 568–80 and throughout). The nomenclature varied, but the scheme itself remained stable for centuries.

presumption of guilt [*violenta praesumptio*] lies against him."[122] Light or probable presumptions were grounds for investigation (and often torture), but not for conviction. Violent presumptions, on the other hand, led directly to conviction because they arose from situations in which (as Bracton put it) the suspect "cannot deny the death nor is further proof necessary."[123] In Cosin's sixteenth-century reiteration of the general principle, which most authorities accepted, "*indicia indubitata* or violent presumptions may serve for full proofe," especially in "hidden crimes, and al such, as (in their owne nature) be of difficult proofe." The "partie may thereupon alone, be . . . condemned."[124]

For some demonologists, even the most common evidence of witchcraft could produce violent presumptions: for Bodin, for instance, witches' marks, the absence of real tears, a gaze fixed on the ground during interrogation, lying, threatening, having spent time with convicted witches, or being a reputed witch.[125] But generally only extraordinary, particularly damning evidence gave rise to them. Such evidence often appeared in the form not of verbal testimony but of material objects, commonly referred to as "permanent facts" because they were not as evanescent as verbal testimony.[126] But sometimes it appeared in the form of visible action: De Lancre claims that he bases his book, in part, on "violent presumptions . . . performed in our presence," which "the legal counselors call *juris et de jure*."[127] Del Río draws a parallel between the classic case of the bloodstained sword and a violent presumption of witchcraft: in the classic case, "everyone says [they] saw the defendant, fearful, pale-faced, and carrying a blood-stained sword, leaving a house in which a murdered man has been found"; similarly, in a witchcraft case, the defendant might be "seen running away, pale-faced, with an instrument of harmful magic from a place in which a person . . . hurt is found, or something which has been bewitched." According to leading jurists, "this is sufficient warrant for condemnation.[128] In cases of witchcraft, physical evidence, suddenly discovered

---

122 Bracton, *De legibus*, 2:386. For Bracton on "presumptions," see, for instance, 2:343, 2:404, 3:147, 4:320.

123 Bracton, *De legibus*, 2:386. See, similarly, Institoris, *Malleus*, 221B (*Hammer*, 569); Bodin, *De la démonomanie*, 417; Boguet, *Discours* (1602), 181; Coke, *First Part of the Institutes*, fol. 6v (Bk. 1, Ch. 1, Sect. 1).

124 Cosin, *Apologie*, 2:63.

125 Bodin, *De la démonomanie*, 318, 395–400. For Bodin, violent presumptions serve as full proof only for non-capital convictions, but they do allow the judge to take measures likely to lead to a "natural death," such as lashing, cutting, branding, perpetual imprisonment, and more. See e.g. Bodin, *De la démonomanie*, 402, 413–15, 417.

126 See e.g. Bodin, *De la démonomanie*, 392, 419 ("faict permanent"); and Cosin, *Apologie*, 2:105 ("*facta permanentia*").

127 Lancre, *Tableau*, ẽ2r (*On the Inconstancy*, 3, translation modified).

128 Del Río, *Disquisitionum*, 41 (Bk. 5, Sec. 5, no. 10; *Investigations*, 205), identifying this as the common view and citing the Italian jurist Prospero Farinacci, though Del Río himself thinks such a case would merely warrant torture.

or displayed, might play the role of the "bloodie hand": wax figures designed to cast a spell; frogs or lizards found in the witch's pockets, under her doorstep, or fed in pots; "human members, especially of small children."[129] As Bodin writes, "[if] the Witch is seized with toads, or lizards, or Hosts, [or] bones, [or] unknown greasy ointments, . . . such presumptions are very violent and urgent."[130]

The word "violent" technically denoted the strength of the presumptions (*violentus*, forcible, vehement).[131] But it also evoked the violence that officials could use to discover such presumptions and (in many cases) shock the accused into confession. Institoris had explained that one must strip witches to find "any device for sorcery that may have been sewn into [their] clothing" and shave all of their bodily hair, for "they sometimes keep superstitious amulets . . . in their clothing or in the hair of the body or sometimes in the most secret places, which cannot be named."[132] So, for instance, when Justice of the Peace Clement Sisley had women strip search "Mother Arnold" (Cecilia Glasenberye) in 1574, they ripped off her hat and allegedly "found . . . swines dung, the herb cherwell[,] dill, red fenell, . . . saint Johns woort, [and] the right hand or forefoote of a Moulewarp" (a mole) "wrapped in a linnen cloth" between "her kercheif and her hat," which "so stanck that no person could abyde it." Upon that discovery, she fell to her knees and begged to keep some: at once a confession (the pamphlet implies) and evidence that she was determined to continue her criminal practices.[133]

If the searching of "secret places, which cannot be named" took place behind closed doors, participants could stage modified violent strip searches quite publicly and dramatically. For instance, according to one pamphlet, Sir Gilbert Gerard supposedly mounted a surprise attack during the trial of Mother Waterhouse after she told him that she could not conjure her familiar:

> 'Agnes waterhouse when dyd thye Cat suck of thy bloud?'
> 'Never,' saide she.
> 'No?' saide hee, 'let me se.'
> And then the jayler lifted up her kercher on her heade and there was diverse spottes in her face & one on her nose.
> 'Then,' sayde the quenes atturney, 'in good faith Agnes when dydde he sucke of thy bloud laste?'
> 'By my fayth, my lorde,' sayde she, 'not this fortnyght.'
> And so the jurye went together for that matter.[134]

[129] For examples of these, see Bodin, *De la démonomanie*, 75, 276, 277, 280–1, 402, 415, 419.
[130] Bodin, *De la démonomanie,* 415.
[131] See, for instance, Institoris, *Malleus*, 222C (*Hammer*, 571).
[132] Institoris, *Hammer*, 545, 552.
[133] *World of Wonders*, sig. E3v (generally attributed to Thomas Johnson). This appears to have been a bone-ache remedy: see Gibson, *Early Modern Witches*, 149.
[134] Phillips, *Examination*, sig. A7v. I have modified punctuation, capitalization, and line breaks in this passage for clarity.

Those attempting to produce *indicia indubitata* demonstratively might do so through an extended demonstration of the kind Jean Grenier's evidentiary expedition promised, hoping that presumptions would accrue cumulatively until they became sufficiently "pregnant." Or they might attempt to do so through a single moment of violently revelatory dramatic action (an *anagnorisis* of sorts), as Sir Gilbert or Jean did. As Boguet points out, surprise staging might function not just as revelation for spectators: it could also shock a witch into confession. The judge should make the sorcerer "so surprised that he does not know where he is, and thus . . . drag the truth out of him."[135] The judges in the trial of the Marlou witches in 1582–3 repeatedly used such surprise confrontations to force confession, relying on the talents of young Bernard Girault to produce sudden, shocking effects. Brought face-to-face with Guillemette Piron (who had allegedly bewitched him), he was "suddenly completely transported, . . . his face ferocious, his eyes reversed in his head." With "a crackling and bitter voice, gnashing his teeth, [he] cried: 'I mounted you!'" and then "with great force and fury, he threw himself on her." Terrified, she began to recite the magic charm: "'I command you in the name of God, to leave the body of this child!'" When that had no effect, she asked if she could beg the devil to stop tormenting the boy: effectively a confession.[136]

For many early moderns, the principal biblical example – and precedent – for the doctrine of violent presumptions was the Judgment of Solomon.[137] As Cosin explains:

> That such *indicia indubitata* or violent presumptions may serve for full proofe in matters of very difficult proofe, we have an example in *Scripture* of *Salomon*; whose wisedome is therefore highly commended, because he grounded his judgement (whether of the two women that contended, was the true mother) upon the motherly pitie which he found in her, that would rather forgoe her naturall childe, then to see it dismembred and parted in twaine.[138]

For Cosin, Solomon resolves a matter "of very difficult proofe" through creative scenography: the staging of a surprise, with a threat of extreme legal violence whose purpose is to trick the participants into revealing themselves. The scene that Cosin references functions almost emblematically: the king commands his servants, "Bring me a sword," raises it as if to strike the child, and the true mother cries out, "Oh my lorde, give her the living childe, and slay him not."[139]

135 Boguet, *Discours des sorciers*, 170.

136 Jacques-Chaquin and Préaud, *Sorciers*, 107–8. Bernard says, "Je t'ai jardi," literally "I gandered you," as a gander does to a goose.

137 See, for instance, Bodin, *De la démonomanie*, 391 (arguing that violent presumptions are founded on natural reason). It is notable that the principal biblical examples of these performative evidentiary doctrines all involve criminal "harlots" (Tamar, the Woman Taken in Adultery, and, here, the "harlo[t]" who is the false mother) (1 Kings 3:16 [fol. 133v]).

138 Cosin, *Apologie*, 2:63–4.

139 1 Kings 3:24–6 (fol. 134r).

Here, violent presumptions are (as Cosin writes of notorious facts) "*made to appeare judicially in Actes unto the Judge*": the judge employs a palpable fiction to conjure circumstantial evidence that appears to reveal the transparent truth.

Cotta criticized the "conjuration" of circumstantial evidence through the "fantasticall ... raising up of their likenesse, and shadows ... out of meere fancy" (a practice that sounds dangerously like witchcraft or, of course, theater).[140] But early modern judges did employ such conjuration, staging fictions whose function was to reveal guilt in a theatrical moment of terror and revelation. Bodin recommended using "shrewd and very skilled spies" to perform undercover in prisons, playing the part of fellow prisoners accused of witchcraft, "and in this way draw forth [the witch's] confession." Such undercover actors could also play the part of torture victims to terrify the accused into confession. As the judge informs the accused that "they are administering the torture," from inside the torture chamber the actor begins to "cry out with a dreadful cry, as if he were in torment."[141] Here, a "fantasticall ... conjuration" – a piece of judicial artifice – could produce the ultimate in "inartificial" proofs: confession. But even where such staging produced only violent presumptions, these bore within them the implicit logic of the doctrine of *indicia indubitata* itself: the word "*indubitata*" both acknowledged doubt (*someone* has doubted) and claimed to answer it dispositively. The doctrine, in this sense, in itself defied the skeptics: you may doubt, but see this and doubt no more!

3 Doing Battle with Satan in a Louviers Courthouse: Devil versus Law in the Trial of Françoise Fontaine (1591)

3.1 The Haunted House, the Servant, and the Reluctant Magistrate

In Louviers, France, in 1591, a genteel family moves into a haunted house. The family has heard an evil spirit in the back rooms: moaning, cooing, sometimes appearing in the form of a pigeon. One day it comes down the chimney "like a brand of fire," overturns tables and chairs, throws furniture out the window onto the street, and generally causes mayhem.[142] Surmising that "sorcery and enchantment" are involved, authorities arrest a suspect: Françoise Fontaine, a twenty-two-year-old servant recently rescued from poverty who is behaving very oddly (5–6). Loys Morel – Sieur de la Tour, Counselor to the King, and Royal Magistrate (*Prévôt*) of the Province of Normandy – takes the case in

[140] Cotta, *Triall*, 97.

[141] Bodin, *De la démonomanie*, 362 (translation in part from Bodin, *On the Demon-Mania*, 179). See, similarly, Boguet, *Discours des sorciers*, 171–2 (*Examen*, 215); and Institoris, *Malleus*, 217A–B (*Hammer*, 558).

[142] Bénet, *Procès*, 3–4 (the principal record of the case, hereafter cited in the text).

hand, proceeding to oversee a nearly month-long trial before crowds of officials, clerics, doctors, visiting dignitaries, guards, prisoners, and members of the general public.

Unlike (for instance) Rémy, Boguet, or de Lancre, Morel is decidedly skeptical that witchcraft is at work. He demands that a doctor, surgeon, and apothecary examine Françoise: Perhaps her strange behavior has natural causes? The kind of magistrate whom people like Galis accused of "winking" at witches, he is ready to acquit, for (as he explains) he really has "n[o] wish to punish her." If he truly believed her guilty he would already have had her hair removed and shaved her body, "as is customary when witches are put on trial." If she will explain herself, he will release her (31). But strange things happen in the courtroom, judicial chambers, and attached prison. Françoise thrashes on the ground so violently that half a dozen men can barely hold her down, "throw[ing] herself here and there" (27). Her hair stands on end, her arms and legs twist, her eyes pop out, her mouth grimaces unnaturally. She also repeatedly appears to levitate, float horizontally across the courtroom floor, rise several feet in the air, and then move on her back "the length of the said courthouse," all apparently unaided by human hands (29).

Still determined not to jump to conclusions, Morel and a conscientious clerk named Vauquet record the case as it proceeds, producing an exhaustively detailed, minute-by-minute *Procès verbal*, or trial record. Unlike lurid entertainments such as *News from Scotland*, the *Procès verbal* is an official legal record not meant for the public eye. It records the unfolding of the trial matter-of-factly, without editorializing or literary flourishes. It is clear from both style and substance (as well as the official nature of the document) that Morel and Vauquet were describing effects they actually thought they saw and heard.[143]

3.2 Possession or Witchcraft?

Morel's skepticism cannot withstand the manifest evidence. This is no natural illness, says the doctor: "sorcery and enchantment" are clearly at work (5, 29). The only issue the court must now decide is whether Françoise is possessed or a witch: if the former, she is an innocent victim; if the latter, she is guilty of the

[143] The *Procès verbal* remained unpublished until Bénet's edition in 1883. As Bénet notes, the text appears as a rapid, unmediated record of the facts, with no attempt at literary elaboration (xii–xiii). Most of the supposedly supernatural events that Vauquet records are in fact easily explicable. Some are similar to those that faux-demoniacs like William Sommers or Anne Gunter later confessed to counterfeiting (though Françoise appears not to have been counterfeiting but merely unconsciously replicating the symptoms of witchcraft). Morel's and Vauquet's perceptual expectations may explain the rest. On Sommers's and Anne Gunter's techniques, see Harsnett, *Discovery*, 182–3, 212–14 (and throughout); and Sharpe, *Bewitching*, especially 7–13.

crime of crimes and must burn. Technically, there was a clear distinction between witch and demoniac (both in England and on the Continent). "[T]he Witch denieth God upon knowledge, and deliberation, wittingly and willingly," explains Perkins; witches "betake themselves to the devill, of their own accord," with both knowledge and consent.[144] Demoniacs, on the other hand, were unwilling victims of the devil, fighting him with all their force (in conflicts they often acted out vocally and physically in their fits: "no, no, I will not. The Lord hath flatly forbidden it in his word[!]")[145]

However, it was not always so easy to tell witch and bewitched apart. Ventriloquizing the devil, replicating his attacks on the godly world, the possessed could seem to metamorphose into diabolical beings. They performatively replicated the witch's well-known wantonness (in mimic pregnancy), the diabolical world of night flight or magic circles (bending their bodies into hoops), and the general inversion of the world order (twisting themselves backwards, reversing their eyes in their heads). They "act[ed] Witchcraft before us, by the motion of [their] bod[ies]" (in the words of one seventeenth-century accuser).[146] Was the demoniac perhaps complicit in the work of the devil? Had she become one with the evil spirit who inhabited her? Judges often struggled to decide. The case of Rollande du Vernois, a young Savoyard woman whom Boguet prosecuted for witchcraft in 1598, offers a classic example.[147] Boguet was hesitant to condemn an innocent but also determined not to allow a witch to escape punishment. In his private chambers, where he and another judge examined her to decide her fate, she suddenly pointed to her stomach where "the evil spirit . . . was possessing her" and then "fell to the ground and began to bark like a dog at the Judge, rolling her eyes in her head with a frightful and horrifying look," "yelp[ing] and yowl[ing]." Clearly a victim of possession. But then she confessed to having succumbed to the devil and made "signs with her head and two fingers that Satan had twice known her carnally."[148] Clearly a witch: guilty.

Morel finds Françoise's case harder to resolve. In her fits, she appears to be a classic victim of possession (as described in both the Bible and contemporary accounts).[149] But her fits also associate her with the world of witchcraft, an

---

[144] Perkins, *Discourse*, 250. [145] *Most Wonderfull and True Storie*, 30.

[146] Boyer and Nissenbaum, *Salem*, 1:84 (Samuel Braybrook describing Bridget Bishop).

[147] See Boguet, *Procès inédits*, 13–22; and his *Discours des sorciers*, 141–50. Boguet argues against exonerating all who show symptoms of possession: if one did, all accused witches would pretend to be possessed to avoid condemnation. For examples of other demoniacs prosecuted as witches, see Levack, *Devil*, 202–5.

[148] Boguet, *Discours des sorciers*, 142, 144 (*Examen*, 173–4).

[149] For useful catalogs of the repertoire of possession (in the Bible and contemporary accounts), see Almond, *Demonic Possession*, 27–8; and Levack, *Devil*, 6–15. For Françoise's similar symptoms, see Bénet, *Procès*, 26, 55, 60–1, 68–9, 72.

identification she appears to intensify symbolically through their specific choreography. She mimics diabolical inversion by crawling upside down or turning "her eyes . . . inside out in her head." She repeatedly falls on her face or appears to have been "thrown . . . from a height," dramatizing her downward fall (both her fallen condition and her link to the underworld). At one point, she throws herself into a well, "head downward, feet in the air," grasping the pulley to prevent herself from "falling into the depths" (68, 48, 54) and yet seemingly hell bound. In such moments, Morel "fea[rs] that the said Françoise is [indeed] a witch" (28–9).

3.3 Confession: Coercion or Consent?

Françoise's eventual confession confirms his fears: as she tells the court, she has in fact willingly given herself to the devil. She has had sex with him repeatedly (ten or twelve times in the very prison itself). As a pledge of her fealty, she has given him her hair, which he has twisted around his finger. Two years hence, she will go with him and not come back (40–41, 93, 47–8). Confession to having made a pact with the devil (a capital offence in most of Europe even in the absence of *maleficium*) is the "queen of proofs."[150] By any contemporary standard, Françoise's confession – made without torture and "of her own accord" ("de soy mesme," as the *Procès verbal* repeatedly stresses [47; and see 42, 43, 45]) – should lead quickly to a guilty verdict. But somehow it does not seem to resolve the question of Françoise's guilt. Perhaps this is because Morel is so reluctant to find her guilty. But perhaps it is also because her confession itself seems to call into question the basic assumptions on which the crime of witchcraft rests.

That confession begins not with the devil but with the story of an all too real recent event. One evening, Françoise was carrying flour to a baker to make bread when three soldiers accosted her. At first they declared her a prostitute and demanded her services. She protested that she was "a good girl" and "a poor servant who earned her livelihood by working in the vineyards." They insisted on walking her to her lodgings, and then claimed that they needed someone to "make their bed" in their room. With the landlady's encouragement, they persuaded her not to be afraid for they would not harm her. Once she was in their room, they announced that if she refused sex or resisted, they would take her to the guardhouse and have her "ridden" by more than three hundred soldiers. She was terrified, and (as she explains) "abandoned herself to the soldiers." The next morning, she was in despair, believing that she had been "given to the Devil" (33–5).

[150] Peters, *Torture*, 41; Krause, *Witchcraft*, 21. The devil's pact was soon to become a capital offense even in England with the institution of the witchcraft act of 1604.

In her account of what the devil then did to her, which follows soon after, Françoise confusedly replicates the rape narrative, converting her sense of this-worldly sexual guilt into a narrative of supernatural legal guilt. The account draws on many of the narrative conventions for stories of diabolical seduction but also mixes in personal details, including violently realistic sexual details.[151] While the devil sometimes wears his traditional black, he is also sometimes dressed in tan (like many sixteenth-century French soldiers) (44, 48). Like the soldiers, he at first offers to pay her. Like them, he takes her into a small room, kissing her and offering "words of love," saying that "he ha[s] to have her company." Like them, he then throws her onto the bed and threatens that if she does not have sex with him he will subject her to worse. He asks her: "Do you not know that you gave yourself to me . . . when the three soldiers took you?" She wants to flee, as from the soliders, but instead, terrified, she consents to his demands (33–4, 38, 41).

The interrogators are quite clearly interested in details that might determine whether or not she consented: they ask her, for instance, "how [the devil] had her company and whether it was he or she who tucked up her chemise" (41). In both narratives, her answers repeatedly blur the lines not only between the soldiers and the devil but between subjection to violence and consent: yes, one of the soldiers had her three times but by then she had already been dishonored; yes, she eventually "agree[d] to go with [the devil] whenever he wants" but by then she "didn't know what to do because she had [already] given herself to him and had his company" (34, 47). Both narratives seem to challenge the distinction between the coerced and the freely willed, triggering a set of questions at the heart of the crime of witchcraft: What is coercion? What is consent? What is free will? What, really, is the difference between possessed victim and criminal witch? Both narratives, that is, offer a kind of implicit critique of "wittin[g] and willin[g] consent," the key juridical concept on which the crime of witchcraft rests and on which Françoise's trial turns.

3.4 Battle with the Devil

What happens after Françoise's confession are a series of events in the courtroom – a crowded auditorium – that subject Morel and his associates to something like the terror she experienced, giving them a taste of what the threat

151 The devil has "ung membre viril fort dur & noir, & de telle grosseur que lad. respondante en enduroit grande douleur, . . . par ce que sond. membre estoit dur comme un caillou & fort froid . . .. [L]ed. grand homme avoit esté longtemps sur elle, il jettoit quelque chose dans son ventre qui estoit froid comme glace, qui venoit jusques au dessus de l'estomac & des tétins de lad. respondante. . . . [I]l avoit grande peyne de retirer son membre viril de la nature de lad. respondante"; they were "prins par la nature, comme ung chien & une chienne" (42; and see 43–44).

of violence may do to one's ostensible freedom of will.[152] Perplexed by Françoise's case, Morel nevertheless begins the trial cockily confident of his powers. He knows just what to do "to prevent a witch from harming others": "one must take a new broom of wood of birch and beat the said witch with it," as he proceeds to do (28). He also knows just how to take on the devil. During her public confession, Françoise turns to an invisible-inaudible spirit who appears to be speaking to her behind her back: clearly the devil. Morel cries out:

> Devil, by the power that I have, as judge established by the King, having the Justice of God in my hand to punish evildoers, I command you to leave the body . . . of the said François[e], and address yourself to me: . . . tell me what you want of her [!] (40)

Demanding that the devil face him like a man (or something like), Morel declares his power – under the aegis of the king and the law – to mete out punishment not only to the king's human subjects but to the Criminal of Criminals, the devil himself. He grandiloquently declares: "neither [the devil] nor any other evil spirit ha[s] any power over the law nor [those] in the hands of the law" (40).

But just beneath the surface of such bravado, it turns out, lie fear and trembling. This becomes apparent in a scene early in the trial in which, attempting to arm themselves against the evil spirit (who appears to be thrashing around inside Françoise's body), Morel and his associates plan a surprise attack:

> [A]dvised that the Gospel of John had a great deal of power against devils, we decided to recite it to her; and for fear that the said Françoise would perceive what we were about to do, we covered our faces with our cloaks, to just below the eyes, [and] approached the said Françoise. (27)

To fend off any evil spirits who might be lurking, they repeatedly cross themselves before and behind as they approach her, reciting: "*Initium sancti Evangelii secundum Johanem. In principio erat Verbum*" ("The Gospel according to John begins: 'In the beginning was the Word'"). As this marching phalanx of chanting judges cloaked up to the eyes draws near, they see a strange sight: "the body of the said Françoise . . . on the ground, . . . her arms extended like a cross, beg[inning] to drag itself along the ground, her head before her [with] her hair bristling." Drawing still nearer, they see her "elevated three or four feet above the ground [and] carried the length of the courtroom." Suddenly, her body comes flying straight toward them. Terrified, they flee into the adjoining room

[152] The trial is in "la cohue," eventually described as the "auditoire de la cohue" (1, 64). "Cohues" seem originally to have been judicial assemblies in castles or near prisons. The word came to designate a noisy crowd ("assemblée bruyante"), presumably because judicial assemblies were large and noisy. See "cohue" in the CNRTL (Lexicographie), https://www.cnrtl.fr/definition/cohue (accessed August 1, 2023).

and slam the door. But Françoise's body follows them and begins to "knock against the door . . . with the soles of its feet," finally flying headfirst out the door of the courthouse and into the horrified crowd (27–8).

Things are soon to get even weirder. Night has fallen. All is momentarily calm. But then, suddenly, Françoise is thrown to the floor "as if . . . from a height," the candles go out, and there is "a great noise." Everyone has fled (thinks Morel), leaving him alone with Françoise in the pitch-black courthouse. In the darkness, he cries out, "My God, grant me the grace never to lose my spirit" and then, "Devil, I command you, by the power that I have as judge[!]" Conjuring the devil when you are alone in the dark turns out to be a bad idea: at that instant, he finds himself "seized by the legs, body and arms." It must be the devil! He hears Françoise cry out as several blows strike her, and then feels himself beaten on the calves with something hard. A violent blow cuts Morel across the face, "from above the ear to the chin the length of the jawbone." He belatedly remembers that he is wearing his sword and tries to pull it out, but he now has a great gash on his wrist, and something has seized his right arm. He cries out again: "Devil and evil spirit, . . . speak to us and tell us what [you] deman[d][!]" But instead of speaking, it jumps on his back and takes him by his lower legs. Breaking his hand free, he swings his sword about in the darkness, but there is no one there. At last, help arrives with torches. As the light spreads across the floor, they find Françoise lying wounded with blood everywhere (48–50).

3.5 The Body as Crucifix and Counter-Crucifix

From the distance of four hundred plus years, the scene may appear farcical: blows and swords fly randomly in the darkness; robed officials grab at arms and legs and jump on one another's backs; Françoise's wounds are slight; no one actually dies. But for the participants it clearly signifies a deadly battle with the devil: the judge has lost control of his courtroom; it is not clear whether he or the devil will win. And the question remains: Which side is Françoise on? How could one tell, in the darkness, whether she is fighting on the side of the devil or the law?

One of Françoise's repeated postures captures this uncertainty – and the challenge it poses to law – in particularly dense symbolic form: her production of the figure of the crucifix with her own body by extending "her two arms . . . like a cross" (25). She forms this crucifix only when in a prone position, "on the ground, face upward, . . . thrashing here and there," creating a horizontal crucifix close to the ground (30; and see 25, 26, 27). On several occasions, she seems to rise in the air and then fall on her back again into the position of the cross, which then moves across the courtroom floor as if marking out the entire space (25, 26, 27–8). Bespeaking her fallen condition, this posture seems also to bear a special relationship to the official judicial-religious sign of the cross, in particular the "image of the crucifix that [is] above the judge's elevated seat," presiding over the central courtroom (30).

Morel makes a special point of showing Françoise this crucifix early in the trial. He tells her "that she need not fear to confess her sin" for the court would "have pity on her and save her life." God "would [also] pardon her," he explains,

> since it was God who . . . creat[ed] [us] in His image; for which reason he does not wish to let his creatures perish, so long as they . . . renounc[e] the Devil and as[k] pardon . . .; at which we showed [her] the image of the crucifix. (30)

The placement of the crucifix above the judge's seat, of course, evokes the parallel between Christ the Judge and the worldly judge, God's representative on earth, stressing the link between the theological and the judicial. In pointing out his crucifix to the spectators, Morel illustrates the explicit parallel between crime and sin, judicial mercy and divine mercy, which the cross above the judge's chair illustrates: if Françoise confesses her sin, God will pardon her; if she confesses her crime, the court will pardon her.

Several images suggest that Françoise's formation of a crucifix with her arms was part of the standard repertoire of possession.[153] The posture appears, for instance, in a Jacques Callot print (c. 1620–30) representing a miraculous exorcism in the sanctuary of the Madonna della Fontenuova in Monsummano (Tuscany) (Fig. 3). Behind the possessed woman is the Madonna, floating on a cloud above a crucifix. The woman's arms are spread, as if she is imitating the crucifix behind her. Like Françoise's cross, hers is a fallen cross, her torso leaning toward the church floor. But even as demonic forces drag her down, she levitates (toes pointed, one foot raised), as if striving upward toward the Madonna and the crucifix that is her model. In the struggle between the devil and his enemies, the crucifix lends its shape to the woman's body, urging salvation.

At the same time, there is another struggle at work in the scene, taking place on the horizontal rather than the vertical axis. A powerful guard dominates the foreground, pointing his pike at the scene. Like Morel, he appears to defy the devil with the force of law. But in aiming his pike at the devil, the guard is, of course, also aiming it at the possessed woman. If the woman pledges herself to the devil, the devil will get her soul, but the guard will get her body. While the guard is, of course, the devil's enemy, he also appears here a bit like the devil in the classic psychomachia of so many medieval and early modern images

---

[153] Institoris's insistence that one tie a demoniac naked to the trunk of a cross during an exorcism suggests one possible origin for the posture (*Hammer*, 452).

Figure 3 The Madonna della Fontenuova and her crucifix miraculously cure a possessed woman. Jacques Callot, *The Possessed One* (1620–30). Engraving. Princeton University Art Museum, Bequest of Junius S. Morgan, Class of 1888

and texts: the physical tug-of-war between angel and devil for the body and soul of the dead. Pointing his pike at the woman, the guard also points it at the Madonna (as the devil points his fork in the psychomachia), as if to say "she is mine." The Madonna faces him, offering the crucifix against the pike: not punishment but mercy. Which shall it be? Punishment for the witch or salvation for the devil's victim?

Another image – illustrating a discussion of possession cases in the 1598 edition of Pierre Boaistuau's *Prodigious and Memorable Histories* – similarly

Figure 4 Priest backed by altar with crucifix exorcises possessed woman with demon emerging from her mouth. Pierre Boaistuau, *Prodigious and Memorable Histories* (*Histoires prodigieuses et memorables*) (1598), 1272. Courtesy of the National Library of Medicine

shows a possessed woman who is both levitating and falling, her arms spread (Fig. 4).[154] The discussion of possession cases treats demoniacs as innocent victims of the devil. But in the image, the woman appears wholly demonic, as if the illustrator needs to remind viewers that some demoniacs are in fact witches. As in the Callot image, the relationship between the demoniac's posture and the crucifix in the background represents the struggle over her soul. In its echo of the composition of Last Judgment images, the image reiterates the cosmic conflict that has produced this struggle. It places the illuminated altar, with its statuette of the Crucifixion, on the left, traditionally where Heaven appears in Last Judgment images (to Christ's right, the side of righteousness). It places the demon on the right, traditionally where Hell appears in Last Judgment images (to Christ's left, the *sinister* side). The woman's mouth is, in effect, a Hellmouth from which a demon emerges. The demon here resembles a deformed caricature of the Christ figure on the left: his body black, his arms forming a crooked cross above the possessed woman's head. The woman struggles between the false cross that the

[154] Boaistuau, *Histoires*, 1272. There were various editions of Boaistuau's *Histoires prodigieuses et mémorables* in the sixteenth century. This edition contains sections added by an unnamed editor not long before its publication, including the discussion of possession cases.

demon represents and the true cross on the altar. Pulled to the demonic side, her posture parallels that of the demon: arms in the form of a similar crooked cross, left foot thrust outward, right foot downward, her robe billowing behind in an approximation of the demon's tail. The priest reaches toward her with the wafer and wine, striving to use the holy power of Christ's body and blood to draw her away from the clutches of the devil, as if to say: do not follow the Antichrist who pulls you down to Hellmouth with his false cross; return to the true cross. It is very like Morel's invitation to Françoise as he points to the image of the crucifix above the judge's seat while she "thrash[es]," "face upward," "her two arms ... like a cross": "renounc[e] the Devil" and come instead to Jesus on the cross.

If the priest in the image appears to fail, so does Morel. For his brief homily on the joint legal-theological meaning of the courtroom crucifix does not produce the desired effect. Françoise responds not by rising but by dropping into the position of the fallen cross: a counterimage of Morel's crucifix. Françoise's fallen crucifix – a more dramatic version of those in the Callot and Boaistuau images – both replicates and revises the upright one on the wall. It transforms the bipartite spatial relationship between Christ the Judge and the worldly judge into a tripartite relationship: Christ on the cross, the seated judge, and the prone woman. If the image of Christ above Morel's seat represents the heavenly realm and the seated judge below him the earthly realm, the prone woman below him must represent the diabolical realm. In this, perhaps Françoise's fall before the heavenly crucifix and worldly judge serves as a confession of sorts. But her bodily crucifix also literalizes what Morel has told her: "God ... creat[ed] [us] in his image." Literalizing this idea constitutes a plea of sorts: if in fact God pardons us because he "creat[ed] [us] in his image," and if the court imitates God's mercy, a demonstration that Françoise bears a likeness to the (literal) image of God seems to compel both divine and judicial pardon.

At the same time, buried in this implicit performance of confession, one might also see a challenge. The crucifix in Morel's courtroom – like that in virtually every courtroom in Catholic Europe – is supposed to affirm the court's divinely underwritten right to punish: to mete out worldly violence that (like the Crucifixion) redeems sin. Images regularly stressed the similarity between the Crucifixion and ordinary criminal penalties. Serving as a model for the condemned, the courtroom crucifix tells them: remember Christ's suffering, repent, and God may be merciful.[155] We might see in Françoise's formation of the fallen cross anticipation of her execution and acquiescence to that mandate. But we might instead see in it a protest that declares: look at the image and then look

[155] See Prosperi, *Crime*, for an extended version of the argument that public execution rituals sought to transform the condemned into a Christlike figure who accepts death as a mode of salvation.

at me and you will see that it is not the judge who is like Christ, but me. Does that not make you very like Christ's executioners?

3.6 The Hair in the Plaster

The crucifix reappears in the grand finale of the trial. Having defied the devil (under the banner of God and the king), fought him with sword, holy water, the Gospel of John, and a birch broom, and attempted to exorcise Françoise at least eight times, Morel finally decides that there is only one remedy left: like other accused witches, Françoise must be shaved. In the middle of the courtroom, the barber-surgeon begins to cut her hair, which officials then burn in the bonfire lit for that purpose. Suddenly, she seems to shoot up in the air and fly around the room, "her head below, her feet in the air, yelling and crying strangely" and emitting great quantities of "water and stinking smoke" from under her skirts (68). Crowds are watching through the windows of the courtroom, "falling to their knees and beginning to pray to God" (68–9, 70). Now Françoise herself is crying out, "Cut quickly, Monsieur the Magistrate, all the hair" (69). Morel and the others fall to their knees in prayer. As he begins to get up from "the step at the foot of the judge's seat, above which was the remembrance of the crucifix," Morel discovers something strange: he finds at the "base of the step and running along it a great quantity of hair." This hair is "in the plaster and emerg[es] from it half a foot, its length . . . more than six feet, and half a foot wide" (69).

"[G]reatly astonished" and deeply disturbed, Morel decides that he must interrupt the trial to interrogate the jailor and his wife: no, they say, in the twenty-three years they have managed the courtroom and prison they have never seen such a thing; indeed, it was not there that very morning when they cleaned the steps. The barber attests to the fact that it looks very much like Françoise's hair, and Morel agrees. So they show it to Françoise, and she tells them: not only is it her hair; it is the very hair that the devil twisted around his finger after she gave it to him (70). Somehow, ominously, the hair has migrated from the witch's head and the finger of the devil himself. Menacingly creeping toward the judge's seat, it has grown from a ring finger's length to a monstrous mane, half a foot wide and six feet long. And now it is virtually impossible to remove. It is "deep down in the said plaster, . . . more than three fingers [deep]." They reach in with their fingers, but the plaster resists them. They find that the hair is "so deep that we were forced to have a pick and iron spade brought to remove the said hair" (71).

If this attempt to remove Françoise's hair through forcible penetration is not quite a replay of the rape, it seems to inspire a parallel plan that comes close: instead of removing Françoise's hair from the steps, they will remove it from her person. They will bring back the barber – who has his own sharp tools in place of pick and spade – and this time they will shave *all* the hair from Françoise's body, most notably the hair on her "shameful parts" (71). Even the barber views this proposal as outrageous, refusing to comply until they threaten him with punishment. Françoise resists in the only way she knows how: turning herself again into a projectile and this time shooting her body into the fire. They pull her out, burnt and suffocated, and still "violently beaten and tormented." The barber shaves her underarms (72). But when he raises his knife to begin on her "shameful parts," something miraculous happens. She says "no," and unlike the soldiers or the devil, they stop. She falls to her knees on the step near the judge's seat, clasps her hands in prayer, looks at the image of the crucifix, and renounces the evil spirit (73). And with that double refusal – of the devil and of those who would violate her – she is at once cured and deemed innocent. The trial is over.[156]

But it is not really over. For there is a disturbing remainder: the hair in the plaster, Françoise's hair, the devil's hair, a reminder of what she has refused to yield up to the tools of law. That hair has escaped law's grasp but still haunts the foundations of the courtroom. On the very steps on which the judge ascends toward the crucifix, the symbol of his most sacred mandate, is the grotesque detritus of the diabolical, so like that on woman's shameful parts, embedded in the oozy foundations of the courtroom. Buried in the plaster, it somehow still appears from between the crevices. It turns out that participating in diabolical magic as law, conjuring witches and the devil in the courtroom, one not only risks a battle in which they may win: one may in fact discover that they were always already there.

4 Staging Possession in the Trial of John Samuel: Witchcraft at the Huntington Assizes (1593)

4.1 'The Most Strange and Admirable Discoverie'

In November 1589, nine-year-old Jane Throckmorton began to display signs of a mysterious illness. The only surviving record of the trial – a pamphlet titled *The Most Strange and Admirable Discoverie of the Three Witches of Warboys* (1593), probably written by Jane's father and corrected by Judge Edward Fenner, who presided over the case – describes her "fits." She would sneeze for half an hour straight, "heave up her belly so as none [could] bend . . . or keepe her downe," shake her legs, arms, and head "as if she had been infected with the running paulsie," and

156 In fact, while Françoise went back to work as a servant, Morel continued to investigate, eventually finding witnesses whose fantastical stories confirmed that what he experienced in the case really happened (74–98).

more.[157] After repeatedly examining her and her urine, a Cambridge physician declared that he could find no medical explanation, so it must be witchcraft (sig. A4r). Soon her four sisters, Joan (15), Mary (11), Elizabeth (10), and Grace (8), along with a number of servants, began to show signs of demonic possession. They accused a neighbor, Alice Samuel, of bewitching them, and eventually extended this accusation to Alice's husband John and their daughter Agnes. Over the course of the next three and a half years, the Throckmorton children became local celebrities, displaying their possession to family, neighbors, crowds of curious spectators, and (in April 1593) the judge and jury of the Huntington Assizes. On the day of the trial, Jane's family brought her into the courtroom and "there in her fit . . . set [her] in the Court before the Judge" (sig. O1r).[158] Her fit became a key element of proof, demonstrating both the veracity of her possession and John Samuel's guilt. Partly on the evidence of her courtroom performance, Alice, Agnes, and John Samuel were hanged the next day.

4.2 In the Courtroom: The Body as Evidentiary Object

As we know from descriptions and surviving early modern courtrooms, those who set up the rooms for assize trials – in castles, town halls, and other kinds of public spaces – organized them around a central four-sided well.[159] Different kinds of spectators sat on each side of the well: the judge presided from an

157 *Most Strange and Admirable Discoverie*, sig. A3r. All in-text references to the Warboys case are to this pamphlet (all quotes preceding a signature reference are on the page with that signature). For a detailed account, see Almond, *Witches of Warboys*. While histories of witchcraft routinely cite this as among the most important English cases, it has received little analysis (exceptions include Gasser, *Vexed With Devils*, 37–66; and Witmore, *Pretty Creatures*, 188–190).

158 The ambiguity of one sentence in *The Most Strange and Admirable Discoverie* has caused some to surmise that John Samuel's examination took place not during the trial but during a pretrial examination on April 4th (the day before the trial) (e.g. Almond, *Witches of Warboys*, 181–2; and Syme, *Theatre and Testimony*, 217–18): "Jane continued in her senceles fits . . . til the fourth of April, . . . which day also the said Mistris Jane was brought to Huntington, and there in her fit was set in the Court before the Judge" (sig. O1v). However, given the pamphlet's representation of Jane's in-court possession as part of the jury trial proper, upon rereading it becomes clear that "and there" describes only continuity of place, not time, and that the sentence must merely mean that Jane came to Huntington on April 4th, and that she was set in court in Huntington some time thereafter (an assessment with which Almond now concurs [private communication]). This makes sense of the pamphlet's repeated use of the word "then" to link Jane's fit to the trial testimony that immediately followed, concluding the episode with the words "[a]nd to draw to some ende, the Jury of life and death . . . found all the Inditements *Billa vera*" (sig. O1v–O2v). Details confirm this view: Fenner's order that John Samuel be brought from among the other prisoners to the upper bar near the clerks (sig. O1r); the absence of Joan (whose fits in Huntington on April 4th drew a large audience [sig. N3r–N4v] but who stopped having fits the night before the trial, requiring the Throckmortons to use Jane's fits during the trial proper); the fact that Fenner corrected the pamphlet and then swore to its truth before the Stationers Company in 1593 (Almond, *Witches of Warboys*, 5) (unlikely if it had contained a gross misrepresentation of the sequence of events).

159 On the spatial arrangement of early modern courtrooms, see Smith, *Common-Welth*, 100; and Graham, *Ordering*, 38–40.

elevated platform on one end; the mass of general spectators sat across from the judge on the other end (with the prisoners generally in chains behind them); the jury members sat in boxes on either side of the well. At the center of the room, viewed on all sides by various classes of spectators, was the prisoner whose case the court was to hear, standing at the inner (or "upper") bar. Also at the center of the room were the witnesses for and against the accused.

While much of the Samuels' trial consisted in reading depositions and hearing the testimony of witnesses, Jane's display of possession, which preceded the examination of any of the accused, appears to have been the trial's centerpiece. Placed in the center of the room near the start of the trial, Jane was the sole focus of attention. But rather than being a witness in an ordinary sense, she was an evidentiary object. The pamphlet's use of the passive voice to describe Jane's initial entrance – she was "set in the Court before the Judge" – emphasizes her passivity: the body of evidence her family set before the court was, quite literally, Jane's body.

> [M]any questions were demanded of her, but she answered to none, for [the] divel would not suffer her to speake: her eyes were open, yet such a mist was before th[em], [that] she neither knew, neither did see her father, which was next her. (sig. O1v)

This coma-like stupor (one of the two characteristic modes of possession), signaling simultaneous sensory and cognitive alienation ("she neither knew, neither did see"), served implicitly to verify the evidence of her body: only subjects lie; objects are just themselves. Her initial passivity stood for the principle: I am not performing my possession; I am not an *actor*, merely a puppet.

Throughout the three (and more) years leading up to the trial, determined to offer notorious evidence of the fact, the Throckmortons had repeatedly staged "experiment[s]" whose purpose was to "prove" the Samuels' guilt "many times ... in [the] sight of many" (sig. B2r, D1v). Before assembled witnesses, they had "tryed [experiments] [twenty] times in one houre." If, for instance, they brought Mother Samuel into the Throckmorton house, the children all "started up upon their feet, ... as well as any in the house"; if they took her out of the house, the children "all s[a]nke downe as a stone upon the ground" (sig. E2r). Before witnesses, Jane's uncle, Gilbert Pickering, blindfolded Jane and then invited her to scratch Mother Samuel's hand (which she did), then covered Mother Samuel's hand with his own "to trie what the childe would doe in this extraordinarie passion": "but the childe would not scratch his hand, but felt too and fro upon the bed for that which she missed" (sig. B2v). The Throckmorton family repeatedly displayed the children to prove that they were genuinely possessed. When, for instance, Joan Throckmorton "started and strugled with her selfe, shivering and shaking of her armes and shoulders in that manner, . . . everie bodie perceived easily [that] it was not possible for any so to do of themselves."[160]

4.3 Staging the Charm: Experiment, Diagnosis, and the World Turned Right Side Up

In the courtroom, focusing on John Samuel, Judge Fenner engaged in an experiment whose aim was both to force confession and to cure Jane. "[T]he Judge caused olde *Samuel* to be brought from amongst the other prisoners to the upper barre, . . . where also stoode the saide *Jane*" (sig. O1r). He placed them beside each other in an attempt to demonstrate that, if Jane was the puppet, Samuel was the puppet master.[161] He then explained that Samuel had "a charme made of certaine words": "As I am a Witch, and did consent to the death of the Lady *Cromwel,* so I charge the divell to suffer Mistris *Jane* to come out of her fit at this present." If Samuel "would speak [these words], the child would be well," at once curing Jane, proving Samuel's diabolical power, and getting him to declare in court, "I am a Witch" (sig. O1v). The experiment was a familiar one. The Throckmortons had staged it for observers again and again, most recently the night before in the garden of the Crown Inn. There, Fenner and "a great assembly of Justices and Gentlemen" (sig. N3v) had watched Agnes pronounce the charm, rendering Joan Throckmorton "presently well" (sig. N4r) and serving as experimental proof of Agnes's guilt. The demonstration authenticated the confession; the confession explained the meaning of the demonstration. The very conventionality of the experiment was (tautologically) central to its value as proof.

In court, however, Samuel refused to repeat the charm: he was incapable of relieving Jane, he insisted; the words were ineffectual and he would "not speak them." After failed attempts to persuade him, Fenner declared that he would "incourage" Samuel by pronouncing the words himself. "As I am a Witch, and did consent to the death of the *Lady Cromwel,*" intoned the judge, "so I charge the divell to suffer Mistris *Jane* to come out of her fit at this present." He then invited "others . . . present" to do the same, in an apparent hope that the rhythmic repetition of the incantation would somehow mesmerize Samuel into reciting the spell through sheer imitation. "As I am a Witch," intoned Doctor Francis Dorington, parson of the Throckmorton's parish, "so I charge the divell to suffer Mistris *Jane* to come out of her fit at this present" (sig. O1v). "As I am a Witch, . . ." intoned one upright citizen after another.[162]

---

[160] *Most Strange and Admirable Discoverie*, sig. N3r–N3v.

[161] I follow the pamphlet in referring to John Samuel as "Samuel" throughout.

[162] Squire Throckmorton, his cousin Robert Throckmorton of Brampton, Gilbert Pickering, his brother Henry, John Pickering (a cousin), and Thomas Nut, Vicar of Ellington, gave evidence to

Jane remained unresponsive. Samuel continued to refuse. This "incourage-[ment]" failing, the judge and others began to make "[m]any good and godly prayers . . . for the ease of the childe." Jane "seemed nothing to be moved" until, at Fenner's command, Samuel "pray[ed] unto God for the comfort of the Childe": "when he named God or Jesus Christ, the childes head, shoulders, & armes were sore shaken, and in shew more troubled then before." This "shew" of John's exclusive power to rouse Jane from stupor to mania served as reasonable grounds for a threat: Fenner told Samuel that if he would not speak the words, the court would summarily find him guilty. And so, "at the length" and "with much adoe," he finally said the magic words, "with a loude voyce" and "in the hearing of all that were present." Those words, "being no sooner spoken by the old Witch, . . . the said mistresse *Jane*, as her accustomed order was, wiped her eyes, and came out of her fit" (sig. O1v).

What has happened? Samuel has performed witchcraft in the very courtroom: everyone has seen him *in flagrante*. At the same time, Fenner has made the sheer "evidence of the fact" notorious through an experimental demonstration. (Without explicitly drawing on Cosin's three kinds of super-proof, the pamphlet does draw on the Roman-canon law language of "proofes, presumptions, circumstances" [sig. O1r], suggesting the author's familiarity with Roman-canon evidentiary doctrines.) In reciting the charm, Fenner and his cohort have served effectively as experimental controls or placebos: fixed variables that represent the normal or "naturall" (sig. A3v), proving, by contrast, Samuel's unnatural power. In exclaiming "you see all, shee is nowe well" (sig. O1v), Fenner points to the link between demonstrative proof ("you see all") and physical cure ("shee is nowe well"). Diagnosis and cure are reciprocal here: the diagnosis produces the cure; the cure proves the diagnosis. If the charm itself is simultaneously evidentiary and curative, the confession nested within it – "I am a Witch" – duplicates that conjunction of the evidentiary and curative. Confession is, itself, both evidence and cure: it proves the charge but is at the same time reparative, redeeming the criminal and allowing for the possibility of worldly forgiveness and divine mercy.

Thus, from one perspective, if the goal of the trial is to eradicate witchcraft and restore godly order, Samuel's recitation of the charm has done the trick. Jane "awakening" acts out both her cure and this restoration of order, writ large. As soon as she comes out of her fit,

> seeing her father, [she] kneeled downe, and asked him [*sic.*] blessing, & made reverence to her uncles that stoode neere her: which before she tooke no shew of knowledge: and wondering said: O Lord, father where am I: For that as it

the Grand Jury immediately before the trial (sig. N4v–O1r). It seems likely that the "others then present" included at least some of these men.

> seemed she neither saw nor heard before, nor knew how she was brought into such a presence. (sig. O1v)

If we did not already have a "violent presumption" (or *indicium indubitatum*) in Samuel's recitation of the charm, we do now, captured in the emblematic scene. This moment enacts a correction of witchcraft's familiar world-upside-down inversion, in which the demonic dominates the godly, women rule over men, children over adults. In fact, the Throckmorton girls have spent three years enacting their own domestic version of the world upside-down, dominating their father and uncles, bucking both parental and godly authority, acting like demons, violent and vulgar by turns. Here, Jane suddenly *recognizes* her father and uncles, in yet another moment that shows the link between knowledge and cure (enacted in a heavily symbolic wiping of the eyes). But, more important, she recognizes them as figures of authority ("before she tooke no shew of knowledge" of them), kneels before her father in a demonstration of submission, and bows to her uncles (effectively, also kneeling and bowing to Judge Fenner, who presides on high). Jane's exclamation conflating God and her father ("O Lord, father") captures the essence of this show of "reverence": in kneeling before the worldly representatives of the Judge of Judges ("Our Father"), she performs a simultaneous restoration of paternal, legal, and divine order. The emblematic scene that Jane acts out is not merely *her* "accustomed order" on emerging from a fit but a restoration of *the* "accustomed order," turning the world back rightside-up.

4.4 *Dangerous Mimesis: Chanting as Conjuration*

From another perspective, however, by mobilizing witchcraft (both as evidence of the crime and in the service of its cure), the trial reproduces the very thing it aims to stamp out. "[W]ill[ing] [Samuel] to speake the words" (sig. O1v), Fenner effectively calls upon a witch to perform witchcraft, – to (in fact) conjure the devil in the courtroom. When Samuel refuses, Fenner goes beyond mere virtual magic, reciting the spell himself, momentarily taking on the persona of the witch ("I am a Witch"), and then calling on others present to follow his example. The modeling that the judge hopes will induce Samuel to recite the spell through mesmeric imitation in fact seems to cast a spell over the others present, mesmerizing one after another into reproducing the incantation. As, one by one, upright citizens chant, "I am a Witch, . . . so I charge the divell . . .," "I am a Witch, . . . so I charge the divell . . .," the trial begins to take on a suspicious resemblance to a sabbat. The German-Polish draughtsman Jan Ziarnko's "Description and Illustration of the Witches' Sabbath" (the image accompanying de Lancre's *Tableau of the Inconstancy of Evil Angels and Demons*) (1612) evokes the scene of just such a sabbat: like Judge Fenner, the "Master of ceremonies and governor of the sabbat" (124) sits on an elevated platform

Figure 5 The devil as judge examines a witch and bewitched child. Detail from Jan Ziarnko's "Description and Illustration of the Witches' Sabbath" in Judge Pierre de Lancre's *Tableau of the Inconstancy of Evil Angels and Demons* (*Tableau de l'inconstance des mauvais anges et demons*) (1612), interleaved 118–19. FC6.L2293.612ta (B). Houghton Library, Harvard University

(at once mock-pulpit and mock-seat of judgment), as in so many images of the sabbat, with witch and child-victim before him (Fig. 5).[163]

Here (and in Fenner's courtroom generally), it becomes clear that, instead of law overpowering witchcraft, witchcraft (performatively at least) overpowers law. One might protest that when Fenner recites the spell, he is in fact not performing witchcraft *himself* but doing something more like theater: "counterfeit[ing] . . . professedly, as Stage-Players doe" (in Richard Bernard's words). And one might further protest that we should distinguish good witchcraft from bad: sometimes a homeopathic remedy is necessary to cure an evil. But this is no "counterfeit[ing]" or mere illusion: Fenner is in fact attempting to produce real witchcraft in his courtroom. And, as for good witchcraft, as George Gifford asked, "[W]hat are they but witches [who] have . . . so many charmes & devises to avoide the daungers of witchcraft, or to unwitch"?[164]

[163] See similarly Guazzo, *Compendium*, 18, 25, 42, 115, 118.

[164] Gifford, *Discourse*, sig. I1v.

4.5 "The Musicke of Davids Harpe" and the "Evill Spirit of God"

In a statement often quoted but rarely analyzed, Fenner seems to acknowledge, somewhat abashedly, that he has in fact had to use witchcraft during the trial to bring Jane relief: Jane is "nowe well," he says, "but not with the musicke of *Davids* harpe." The pamphlet explains: the judge is "alluding to the place of Scripture, where King *Saul* being vexed by an evill spirit received comfort and helpe when *David* played on his harpe before him" (sig. O1v). The reference draws, of course, on the typological equations between David and Christ, and between temporal courts and the Last Judgment. One expects law to function as the temporal equivalent of the divine court: just as David's heavenly music purges the evil spirit that vexes Saul, so the heavenly music played at Judgment Day will purge the evil that vexes the world; and so a court of law purges the evil that vexes society, acting in imitation of divine judgment and bringing "comfort and helpe" to the godly.

However, Fenner stresses that, in using the charm, he has cured Jane *not* "with the musicke of *Davids* harpe" but with (by implication) its antithesis. Looking at 1 Samuel 15 and 16 (from which Fenner draws the reference) helps clarify the nature of that implied antithesis. Samuel the Prophet reproaches Saul for disobeying God, disobedience that Samuel equates with witchcraft: "rebellion *is as* the sin of witchcraft," he tells Saul (15:23, fol. 113v).[165] This makes sense since, while one might not normally think of rebellion as witchcraft, witchcraft was certainly treason against God (as many pointed out).[166] As Saul's punishment, not only does God withdraw the "Spirit of the Lorde" from him: He sends "an evill spirit" to "ve[x]" Saul. Observing Saul now essentially possessed ("[b]ehold nowe, the evill spirit of God vexeth thee"), his servants offer "to seeke a man, that is a cunning player upon the harpe: that when the evill spirit of God commeth upon thee, he may play with his hand, and thou mayest be eased" (16:14–16, fol. 114r). The "cunning" man they send for is, of course, David. When "the evill spirite of God" again possesses Saul, David "tooke an harpe and played with his hand, and Saul was refreshed, and was eased: for the evill spirite departed from him" (16:23, fol. 114r).

In the context of a witch trial, spectators would have understood Judge Fenner's allusion to the story of Saul and David as also referencing its

---

165 Unless otherwise noted, all biblical references here are to 1 Samuel, with chapter and verse followed by the volume's folio number.

166 See e.g. Perkins, *Discourse*, 248–9.

sequel: the story of Saul and the Witch of Endor. Early moderns often cited Saul's consultation with the Witch of Endor as inarguable proof of the existence of modern witches. Just like modern witches, the Witch of Endor had "a familiar spirite" (28:7, fol. 119v) and was to be consulted by night; "goe not with *Saule* the reprobate to aske cou[n]saile of [witches]," urges one 1579 pamphlet.[167]

Like Judge Fenner, Saul presents himself officially as an enemy of witchcraft: he has engaged in a campaign to eradicate it, "destroy[ing] the sorcerers, and the soothsayers out of the land" (28:9, fol. 119v). But he is irresistibly drawn to their magic. As a young man – in an episode that presages his consultation with the Witch of Endor – he joins a band of ecstatic prophets (effectively soothsayers), wandering the countryside "with a viole, and a tymbrell, & a pipe, and an harpe before them" (10:5, fol. 111 r). Later, several groups of messengers whom Saul sends to kill David fall under the spell of another such band. When Saul finally goes to see what has happened, he falls under their spell himself: "And he stript off his clothes, and he prophecied also, ... and fell downe naked all that day and all that night" (19:24, fol. 116 r).[168] Given the association of Saul with witchcraft, this scene surely evoked the sabbat for early moderns: Saul's ecstatics "stri[p] off [their] clothes" and "fal[l] downe naked" all day and all night; Pierre de Lancre's "danc[e] completely naked" day and night "to the tune of violins, trumpets, or tambourines" (as in Jan Ziarnko's portrayal [Fig. 6]).[169] Finally, in perhaps the most famous scene of witchcraft in the Bible, Saul visits the Witch of Endor in disguise, commanding her to use her "familiar spirite" to conjure a soothsayer – Samuel the Prophet – from the dead (28:8, fol. 119v). Like John Samuel, she at first refuses, thinking the command is an attempt to entrap her into an illegal performance of witchcraft and that she will be executed for it: "Beholde, thou knowest what Saul hath done, how hee hath destroyed the sorcerers, and the soothsayers out of the land: wherefore then seekest thou to take mee in a snare to cause me to die?" (28:9, fol. 119v). But Saul insists, and she becomes the instrument enacting his witchcraft.

Judge Fenner cites the passage on David's musical exorcism of Saul as a biblical analogue for the victory over malign possession that he has just produced in his courtroom (effectively, an exorcism, without the Catholic connotations). David's harp is like the "charme" not only because they both exorcise possession but also because they are both forms of aural expression

[167] *Rehearsall Both Straung and True*, sig. A3r; and see Cotta, *Triall*, 31, 55, 84.

[168] The identification of divination, soothsaying, and prophesy as witchcraft was common: see, for instance, Perkins, *Discourse*, 56–126, and Cotta, *Triall*, 55–58.

[169] Lancre, *Tableau*, 126, 128.

Figure 6 Witches "danc[e] completely naked" to a "harpe," "pipe," lute, "trumpe[t]," and "viole." Detail from Jan Ziarnko's "Description and Illustration of the Witches' Sabbath" in Judge Pierre de Lancre's *Tableau of the Inconstancy of Evil Angels and Demons* (*Tableau de l'inconstance des mauvais anges et demons*) (1612), interleaved 118–19. FC6.L2293.612ta (B). Houghton Library, Harvard University

whose power lies not in reference but in performative effectuality. Perhaps Fenner thought of the passage not only because it references "witchcraft," the "vex[ations]" of possession, and dispossession, but also (through a set of seemingly more random associations) because the story features a man named "Samuel" and a "cunning" man who is also a "neighbor."[170]

However, both the passage itself and Fenner's identification of it with the scene at hand appear to blur the distinctions between good and evil, witchcraft and godly cure. Rather than setting up an opposition between God and the evil spirit, the passage aligns them: it is "the evill spirit of God" that torments Saul (the phrase, repeated, suggests that the evil spirit is not just sent by God, but is somehow *His* evil spirit).[171] Rather than setting up an opposition between the neighborhood cunning man and the Christ figure, it makes them one: the cunning man *is* in this case, David, the shepherd of Bethlehem, Saul's savior, who comes with "an asse *laden* with bread, and . . . wine" (16:20, fol. 114r) (progenitor, of course, of another Savior shepherd of Bethlehem bearing bread and wine). In the application of the biblical parallel, the implied contrast between healing "with the musicke of *Davids* harpe" and healing "*not* with the musicke of *Davids* harpe" begins to collapse. As early modern images suggested by routinely portraying a demon figurehead on David's harp (as if to capture his music's alliance with the "evill spirite" it ostensibly exorcises), divine music and witchcraft may be one.[172]

I do not wish to overstate the parallels here. What happens after the Witch of Endor yields to Saul's command and performs her magic is not a cure for possession (as in Judge Fenner's courtroom), and it generates a scene that is the diabolical reverse of the kind of godly prayer inherent in Jane's corrective performance. When the Witch of Endor performs her magic, "gods ascen[d] up out of the earth" and Saul "encline[s] his face to the ground, and bow[s] himselfe" (28:13–14, fol. 119v), in what early moderns routinely envisioned as a scene not only of conjuring but of idolatrous devil worship: the false gods and a diabolically produced phantasm of Samuel arise from Hell and Saul bows down to them.[173]

However, the similarities are striking, for in both the biblical story and John Samuel's trial, an enemy of witchcraft orders a witch to perform witchcraft for him and cannot resist, himself, becoming an instrument of witchcraft. If Fenner imagines himself somehow as David, one with the power to dispossess through performance, he is also the accursed Saul: producing magic "not with the musicke of *Davids* harpe" but through the criminal instrumentality of the witch. In this micro-allegorical moment, Saul represents the dissolution of the

[170] Bewitched, Jane experiences "vexations" (sig. O1r). David is Saul's "neighbor" (15:28, 113v).

[171] See also 1 Samuel 18:10, 19:9, fol. 115r–115v.

[172] See e.g. Jean Cousin's illustration of David playing his harp in *Figures de la saincte Bible*, 105; or Erasmus Quellin the Younger's "Saul and David" (1635).

[173] See e.g. Gifford, *Discourse*, sig. C1v; Perkins, *Discourse*, 23–4.

boundary between counter-witchcraft and witchcraft, between the executioner of witches and the witch, between the holy and the blasphemous. If the legal proceeding has made Jane well, it is *not* because it has been like the holy music of David's heavenly harp, bringing "comfort and helpe" to those "vexed by an evill spirit." In fact, what has cured Jane (and, by extension, the community) is bringing the work of the "evill spirit" itself into the courtroom, effectively turning legal ritual into demonic invocation and the courtroom into the devil's domain.

5 Conclusion: Law as Magic

In this Element, I have made two central claims, which may appear to be in tension with each other but are in fact complementary, representing what I view as my two central contributions. On the one hand, I have argued that in witch trials across Europe there was a shared performance repertoire: a common stock of charms, tests, and rituals for the staging of witchcraft that served as proof of guilt. I have argued not only that this shared repertoire acted as evidence but that its specific modes – the performance of witchcraft before legal authorities, the quasi-scientific demonstrations of cause and effect, the staging of scenes of damning revelation – answered to specific doctrines of proof. To point to the breadth of the phenomena I describe, I have invoked a wide array of instances, while showing these phenomena more specifically at work in the trials of Françoise Fontaine and John Samuel. However different those two trials may have been, in both we find participants restaging the crime in the courtroom, testing the veracity and nature of possession through a series of public experiments, revealing witchcraft through a set of violently emblematic scenes.

On the other hand, these two cases remind us how different one trial could be from another. Scholars of witchcraft have long studied such differences when comparing geographies, legal systems, or demographies: Catholic versus Protestant, civil versus common law, female versus male, youth versus age. They have often highlighted the diversity of trials across Europe by contrasting trials that conform to common assumptions (judges determined to convict, confession only under torture or threat, inevitable guilty verdicts, as in John Samuel's trial) with those that challenge such assumptions (judges reluctant to convict, voluntary confession, acquittal, as in Françoise Fontaine's trial). But what I have tried to suggest in my extended readings is that we cannot fully understand the trials by reducing them to geographical or legal or demographic categories, or by looking at judicial attitudes, patterns of confession, or outcomes. Each trial has its own performance dynamics, its own figural threads, its own kinds of narrative unfolding. In each trial there lies a world of irreducible particularities. These can be understood only by attempting to reconstruct events in all their visual, auditory, kinesthetic, spatial, temporal, emotional, and conceptual fullness, – by attending not just to patterns but to contradictions and incongruities.

I have focused on the period in which prosecutions were at their height because this was the period in which longstanding ways of demonstrating witchcraft developed into something like a trans-European, specifically legal, evidentiary performance repertoire. But one can find the kinds of evidentiary performances I have described throughout the period of the witch trials. They appear in nascent form in the *Malleus maleficarum* in the 1480s (as the instances I cite should suggest). And they appear as established conventions in trials throughout the seventeenth century, most famously in the Salem witch trials of 1692–3, where they show up in hyperbolic form in the scenes of frenzied possession collectively choreographed in the courthouse.

If these phenomena were specific to the period of the witch trials, one might nevertheless see them as instances of a much longer history of evidentiary performance. For performance in the name of legal persuasion is as old as law itself, though it may have different aims at different moments. In a medieval witch trial, the accused might request the staging of an ordeal, hoping to display supernatural powers that would demonstrate innocence through divine revelation.[174] In one Lisbon trial in 1690, a Black Cape Verdean freedman named Patrício de Andrade sought to stage his magic tricks for the tribunal to prove that he was not a sorcerer but merely a charlatan.[175] In a trial in London in 1944, the psychic medium Helen Duncan tried to stage a séance for the court to show that she was not a charlatan but in fact a sorceress of sorts, with genuine power over the invisible world.[176]

We might treat Helen Duncan's desire to conjure the voices of the departed in the courtroom as emblematic. For evidentiary performance represents an abiding desire in the history of law to restore the past, to "make the scene live before our eyes" (as Cicero advised the legal orator), to revivify the dead.[177] In this, the courtroom is always a space of conjuring. So it is perhaps not so strange that judges like Loys Morel or Edward Fenner used their courtrooms to conjure the devil or perform curative magic. Law has always sought to render evidence of the invisible world visible, to conjure through the recitation of charms and the

174 See Bartlett, *Trial by Fire and Water*, 23–5, 68–9, 71, 134, 144–52 (on accusations of witchcraft decided by ordeal).

175 See Cook, "Mandinga Experience."

176 Gaskill, *Hellish Nell* (and private communication).

177 Cicero, *Brutus, Orator*, 413 [Orator, 139].

casting of spells.[178] The magicians of the law, with their "cunning tricks and stratagems" (in Institoris's phrase), may try to stay on the right side of the thin edge between law and witchcraft, holy and unholy, executioner and criminal.[179] But as Bodin writes, "by [such] means the Devil makes Witchcraft out of Law." It may be that attempting to use legal magic against the demonic always entails a journey to the other side. It may be that one can never be entirely sure that one is not, in fact, allied with the evil one strives to conquer.

---

[178] See Corcos, *Law and Magic*, for a set of essays theorizing contemporary law as a magical practice.

[179] Institoris, *Malleus*, 199A (*Hammer*, 513).

References

Almond, Philip C., ed. *Demonic Possession and Exorcism in Early Modern England: Contemporary Texts and Their Cultural Contexts*. Cambridge: Cambridge University Press, 2004.

Almond, Philip C. *The Witches of Warboys: An Extraordinary Story of Sorcery, Sadism and Satanic Possession in Elizabethan England*. London: Tauris, 2008.

Ankarloo, Bengt, Stuart Clark, and William Monter. *Witchcraft and Magic in Europe: The Period of the Witch Trials*. Philadelphia: University of Pennsylvania Press, 2002.

Anno primo Reginae Elizabethae. London: Richarde Jugge and John Cawood, 1559 [i.e. 1572?].

Aubrey, John. *Remaines of Gentilisme and Judaisme*. Ed. James Britten. London: W. Satchell, Peyton, and Co., 1881.

Augustine of Hippo. *De civitate dei libre XI–XXII. Aurelii Augustini opera*, pars. 14, vol. 2. [Corpus Christianorum.] Turnhout: Brepols, 1955.

Baddeley, Richard. *The Boy of Bilson: or, A True Discovery of the Late Notorious Impostures of Certaine Romish Priests in Their Pretended Exorcisme, or Expulsion of the Divell out of a Young Boy, Named William Perry*. London: William Barret, 1622.

Bartlett, Robert. *Trial by Fire and Water: The Medieval Judicial Ordeal*. Oxford: Clarendon Press, 1986.

Bénet, Armand, ed. *Procès verbal fait pour délivrer une fille possédée par le malin esprit à Louviers*. Paris: Progrès Médical, A. Delahaye et Lecrosnier, 1883.

Bernard, Richard. *A Guide to Grand-Jury Men … in Cases of Witchcraft*. London: Edward Blackmore, 1627.

The Bible. Translated According to the Ebrew and Greeke, and Conferred with the Best Translations in Divers Languages. [Geneva Bible.] London: Christopher Barker, 1592.

Blackwell, George. *A Large Examination Taken at Lambeth*. London: Robert Barker, 1607.

Boaistuau, Pierre. *Histoires prodigieuses et mémorables: Extraictes de plusieurs fameux autheurs grecs & latins, sacrez & profanes, divisées en six livres*. Paris: Veuve de Gabriel Buon, 1598.

Bodin, Jean. *De la démonomanie des sorciers*. Ed. Virginia Krause, Christian Martin, and Eric MacPhail. Geneva: Librairie Droz, 2016.

On the Demon-Mania of Witches. Trans. Randy A. Scot. Ed. Randy A. Scot and Jonathan L. Pearl. Toronto: Centre for Reformation and Renaissance Studies, 1995.

Boes, Maria R. *Crime and Punishment in Early Modern Germany: Courts and Adjudicatory Practices in Frankfurt am Main, 1562–1696*. Farnham: Ashgate, 2013.

Boguet, Henry. *Discours des sorciers, tiré de quelques procez ... avec une instruction pour un juge en faict de sorcelerie*. Lyon: Jean Pillehotte, 1602.

Discours execrable des sorciers: Ensemble leur Procez, fait depuis 2. ans ... avec une instruction pour un juge, en faict de sorcelerie. Rouen: Romain de Beauvais, 1606.

An Examen of Witches. Ed. Montague Summers. Trans. E. Allen Ashwin. London: J. Rodker, 1929.

Les procès inédits de Boguet en matière de sorcellerie dans la grande judicature de Saint-Claude, XVIe–XVIIe siècles. Ed. Francis Bavoux. Dijon: Bernigaud et Privat, 1958.

Boyer, Paul and Stephen Nissenbaum, eds. *The Salem Witchcraft Papers: Verbatim Transcripts of the Legal Documents of the Salem Witchcraft Outbreak of 1692*. 3 vols. New York: Da Capo Press, 1977.

Bracton, Henry de. *De legibus et consuetudinibus Angliae (Bracton on the Laws and Customs of England)*. [English & Latin: Bracton online]. Harvard Law School Library. 2003. http://amesfoundation.law.harvard.edu/Bracton/.

Bradwell, Stephen. "Mary Glovers Late Woeful Case." In *Witchcraft and Hysteria in Elizabethan London: Edward Jorden and the Mary Glover Case*. Ed. Michael MacDonald. London: Tavistock/Routledge, 1991 (separately paginated).

Briggs, Robin. *Witches and Neighbors: The Social and Cultural Context of European Witchcraft*. New York: Viking, 1996.

Butler, Todd Wayne. "Bedeviling Spectacle: Law, Literature, and Early Modern Witchcraft." *Yale Journal of Law & the Humanities*, 20:2 (2008), 111–29.

Calendar of State Papers Domestic: Charles I, 1634–5. Ed. John Bruce. London: Longman et al., 1864. British History Online http://www.british-history.ac.uk/cal-state-papers/domestic/chas1/1634-5.

Campe, Rüdiger. *The Game of Probability: Literature and Calculation from Pascal to Kleist*. Trans. Ellwood H. Wiggins, Jr. Stanford: Stanford University Press, 2012.

Certeau, Michel de. *La Possession de Loudun*. Paris: Julliard, 1970.

Cicero, Marcus Tullius. *Brutus, Orator*. Trans. G. L. Hendrickson and H. M. Hubbell. Rev. ed. Cambridge: Harvard University Press, 1962.

Clark, Stuart. "'Feigned Deities, Pretended Conferences, Imaginary Apparitions': Scepticism in State Theory and Witchcraft Theory." In *Hexenprozess und Staatsbildung/Witch-Trials and State-Building*. Ed. Johannes Dillinger, Jürgen Michael Schmidt, and Dieter R. Bauer. Bielefeld: Verlag für Regionalgeschichte, 2008, 265–83.

Thinking with Demons: The Idea of Witchcraft in Early Modern Europe. Oxford: Clarendon Press, 1997.

Clubb, Louise George. *Italian Drama in Shakespeare's Time*. New Haven: Yale University Press, 1989.

Coffin, Charlotte A. "Theatre and/as Witchcraft: A Reading of *The Late Lancashire Witches* (1634)." *Early Theatre* 16:2 (2013), 91–119.

Coke, Sir Edward. *The First Part of the Institutes of the Lawes of England*. London: Societie of Stationers, 1628.

Colleton, John. *A Just Defence of the Slandered Priestes*. London: R. Field, 1602.

Cook, Lexie. "The Mandinga Experience: Illusion and Proof in the Inquisition Case of Patrício de Andrade, 1690." *Bulletin of the Comediantes* 74:1–2 (2022), 305–29.

Corcos, Christine A., ed. *Law and Magic: A Collection of Essays*. Durham, NC: Carolina Academic Press, 2010.

Cosin, Richard. *An Apologie for Sundrie Proceedings by Jurisdiction Ecclesiasticall*. 3 Parts [separately paginated]. 2nd ed. London: Printers to the Queen, 1593.

Cotta, John. *The Triall of Witch-Craft*. London: Samuel Rand, 1616.

Dalton, Michael. *The Countrey Justice*. London: Societie of Stationers, 1618.

Damaška, Mirjan R. *Evaluation of Evidence: Pre-Modern and Modern Approaches*. Cambridge: Cambridge University Press, 2019.

Darr, Orna Alyagon. *Marks of an Absolute Witch: Evidentiary Dilemmas in Early Modern England*. Burlington: Ashgate, 2011.

Daston, Lorraine. *Classical Probability in the Enlightenment*. Princeton: Princeton University Press, 1995.

Deats, Sara Munson. "'Mark This Show': Magic and Theater in Marlowe's *Doctor Faustus*." *Placing the Plays of Christopher Marlowe: Fresh Cultural Contexts*. Ed. Sara Munson Deats and Robert A. Logan. London: Routledge, 2016, 13–24.

Del Río, Martín. *Disquisitionum magicarum libri sex*. 3 vols. Louvain: Gerard Rivius, 1599–1600.

Investigations into Magic. Ed. and trans. P. G. Maxwell-Stuart. Manchester: Manchester University Press, 2009.

Dolan, Frances E. *True Relations: Reading, Literature, and Evidence in Seventeenth-Century England*. Philadelphia: University of Pennsylvania Press, 2013.

Duni, Matteo. "Skepticism." In *Encyclopedia of Witchcraft: The Western Tradition*. Ed. Richard M. Golden. 4 vols. Santa Barbara: ABC-CLIO, 2006, 4:1044–50.

Durston, Gregory. *Witchcraft and Witch Trials: A History of English Witchcraft and Its Legal Perspectives, 1542 to 1736*. Chichester: Barry Rose, 2000.

Fairfax, Edward. *Daemonologia: A Discourse on Witchcraft as it was Acted in the Family of Mr. Edward Fairfax . . . in the Year 1621*. Ed. William Grainge. Harrogate: R. Ackrill, 1882.

Figures de la saincte Bible accompagnees de briefs discours, contenans la plus grande partie des histoires sacrées du Vieil & Nouveau Testament. Paris: Jean Le Clerc, 1615 (rpt. 1596).

Fulbeck, William. *A Parallele or Conference of the Civill Law, the Canon Law, and the Common Law of this Realme of England*. [Part 1.] London: Thomas Wight, 1601.

Galis, Richard. *A Brief Treatise Containing the Most Strange and Horrible Cruelty of Elizabeth Stile Alias Rockingham and her Confederates*. London: J. Allde, 1579.

Gaskill, Malcolm. *Hellish Nell: Last of Britain's Witches*. London: Fourth Estate, 2001.

"Witchcraft and Evidence in Early Modern England." *Past and Present* 198 (Feb 2008), 33–70.

"Witches and Witchcraft Prosecutions, 1560–1660." *Early Modern Kent, 1540–1640*. Ed. Michael Zell. Woodbridge, Suffolk: Boydell, 2000, 245–79.

Gasser, Erika. *Vexed With Devils: Manhood and Witchcraft in Old and New England*. New York: New York University Press, 2017.

Gibson, Marion, ed. *Early Modern Witches: Witchcraft Cases in Contemporary Writing*. London: Routledge, 2000.

Reading Witchcraft: Stories of Early English Witches. London: Routledge, 1999.

Rediscovering Renaissance Witchcraft: Witches in Early Modernity and Modernity. New York: Routledge, 2018.

The Witches of St Osyth: Persecution, Betrayal and Murder in Elizabethan England. Cambridge: Cambridge University Press, 2022.

Gifford, George. *A Dialogue Concerning Witches and Witchcraftes*. London: Tobie Cooke and Mihil Hart, 1593.

A Discourse of the Subtill Practises of Devilles by Witches and Sorcerers. London: Toby Cooke, 1587.

Goodare, Julian. *The European Witch-Hunt.* London: Routledge, 2016.

Graham, Clare. *Ordering Law: The Architectural and Social History of the English Law Court to 1914.* Burlington: Ashgate, 2003.

Greenblatt, Stephen. "Loudun and London." *Critical Inquiry*, 12:2 (Winter, 1986), 326–46.

"Shakespeare and the Exorcists." *Shakespeare and the Question of Theory.* Ed. Patricia Parker and Geoffrey Hartman. New York: Methuen, 1985, 163–86.

Guazzo, Francesco Maria. *Compendium maleficarum in tres libros distinctum.* Milan: Haeredes August Tradati, 1608.

Harsnett, Samuel. *A Discovery of the Fraudulent Practises of John Darrel Bacheler of Artes.* London: John Wolfe, 1599.

Heath, James. *Torture and English Law: An Administrative and Legal History from the Plantagenets to the Stuarts.* London: Greenwood, 1982.

Holmes, Clive. "Women: Witnesses and Witches." *Past and Present* 140 (Aug 1993), 45–78.

Homza, L. A. (2022). *Village Infernos and Witches' Advocates: Witch-Hunting in Navarre, 1608–1614.* University Park: Pennsylvania State University Press.

Hopkins, Matthew. *The Discovery of Witches.* London: R. Royston, 1647.

Institoris, Heinrich. *The Hammer of Witches: A Complete Translation of the Malleus Maleficarum.* Ed. and trans. Christopher S. Mackay. Cambridge: Cambridge University Press, 2009.

Malleus Maleficarum von Heinrich Institoris (alias Institoris) unter Mithilfe Jakob Sprengers aufgrund der dämonologischen Tradition zusammengestellt: Widergabe des Erstdrucks von 1487 [facsimile]. Ed. André Schnyder. Göppingen: Kümmerle Verlag, 1991.

Jacques-Chaquin, Nicole and Maxime Préaud, eds. *Les Sorciers du Carroi de Marlou: Un procès de sorcellerie en Berry (1582–1583).* Grenoble: Jérôme Millon, 1996.

James IV and I, King of Scotland and England. *Daemonologie.* Edinburgh: Robert Waldegrave, 1597.

Kamali, Elizabeth Papp. "Finding Facts in Medieval English Law." *Journal of Legal Analysis* 15 (2023), 158–82.

Klotz, Lisa-Jane. "'Suspicion is No Proof': Legal Proof and Probability in Practice and Fiction in Early Modern England." PhD thesis, University of North Carolina, Chapel Hill, 2006.

Kounine, Laura. *Imagining the Witch: Emotions, Gender, and Selfhood in Early Modern Germany.* Oxford: Oxford University Press, 2018.

Kounine, Laura and Michael Ostling, ed. *Emotions in the History of Witchcraft*. London: Palgrave Macmillan, 2016.

Krause, Virginia. *Witchcraft, Demonology, and Confession in Early Modern France*. Cambridge: Cambridge University Press, 2015.

Lancre, Pierre de. *On the Inconstancy of Witches: Pierre de Lancre's Tableau de l'Inconstance des Mauvais Anges et Demons (1612)*. Ed. Gerhild Scholz Williams. Trans. Harriet Stone and Gerhild Scholz Williams. Tempe, Arizona: ACMRS and BREPOLS, 2006.

Tableau de l'inconstance des mauvais anges et demons. Paris: Jean Berjon, 1612.

Langbein, John H. *Prosecuting Crime in the Renaissance: England, Germany, France*. Cambridge: Harvard University Press, 1974.

Torture and the Law of Proof: Europe in the Ancien Régime. 2nd ed. Chicago: University of Chicago Press, 2006.

Larner, Christina. "Crimen Exceptum? The Crime of Witchcraft in Europe." *Crime and the Law: The Social History of Crime in Western Europe Since 1500*. Ed. V. A. C. Gatrell, Bruce Lenman and Geoffrey Parker. London: Europa Publications, 1980, 49–75.

Le Loyer, Pierre. *Discours, et histoires des spectres, visions et apparitions des esprits, anges, demons, et ames, se monstrans visibles aux hommes*. Paris: Nicolas Buon, 1605.

Levack, Brian P. *The Devil Within: Possession and Exorcism in the Christian West*. New Haven, CT: Yale University Press, 2013.

ed. *The Oxford Handbook of Witchcraft in Early Modern Europe and Colonial America*. Oxford: Oxford University Press, 2013.

"Possession, Witchcraft, and the Law in Jacobean England," *Washington and Lee Law Review*, 52 (1995), 1613–40.

The Witch-Hunt in Early Modern Europe. 4th ed. London: Routledge, 2016.

Levine, Laura. *Afterlives of Endor: Witchcraft, Theatricality, and Uncertainty from the "Malleus Maleficarum" to Shakespeare*. Ithaca: Cornell University Press, 2023.

MacDonald, Michael, ed. *Witchcraft and Hysteria in Elizabethan London: Edward Jorden and the Mary Glover Case*. London: Tavistock/Routledge, 1991.

Machielsen, Jan. "The Making of a Teen Wolf: Pierre de Lancre's Confrontation with Jean Grenier (1603–10)." *Folklore* 130 (Sept 2019), 237–57.

Mandrou, Robert, ed. *Possession et sorcellerie au XVIIe siècle: Textes inédits*. Paris: Fayard, 1979.

Maxwell-Stuart, P. G. *Witchcraft in Europe and the New World, 1400–1800*. New York: Palgrave, 2001.

Millar, Charlotte-Rose. *Witchcraft, the Devil, and Emotions in Early Modern England*. New York: Routledge, 2017.

The Most Strange and Admirable Discoverie of the Three Witches of Warboys. London: Thomas Man and John Winington, 1593.

The Most Wonderfull and True Storie, of a Certaine Witch named Alse Gooderige of Stapen Hill. London: n.p., 1597.

Mukherji, Subha. "Knowing Encounters: Law, Legibility and the Rhetoric of Presence in the Early Modern Imagination." Talk ("Law and Poetics" conference, Cambridge, UK), July 2, 2018.

Law and Representation in Early Modern Drama. Cambridge: Cambridge University Press, 2006.

Newes from Scotland . . . With the True Examinations of the . . . Witches, as They Uttered Them in the Presence of the Scottish King. London: William Wright, 1592.

Normand, Lawrence and Gareth Roberts, eds. *Witchcraft in Early Modern Scotland: James VI's Demonology and the North Berwick Witches*. Exeter: University of Exeter Press, 2000.

North, Roger. *The Life of the Right Honourable Francis North*. London: John Whiston, 1742.

Pearl, Jonathan L. *The Crime of Crimes: Demonology and Politics in France, 1560–1620*. Waterloo, Ontario: Wilfrid Laurier University Press, 1999.

Perkins, William. *A Discourse of the Damned Art of Witchcraft*. Cambridge: Cantrel Legge, 1608.

Peters, Edward. *Torture*. 2nd ed. Philadelphia: University of Pennsylvania Press, 1996.

Peters, Julie Stone. "Law as Performance: Historical Interpretation, Objects, Lexicons, and Other Methodological Problems." In *New Directions in Law and Literature*. Ed. Elizabeth Anker and Bernadette Meyler. New York: Routledge, 2017, 193–209.

Law as Performance: Theatricality, Spectatorship, and the Making of Law in Ancient, Medieval, and Early Modern Europe. Oxford: Oxford University Press, 2022.

Phillips, John. *The Examination and Confession of Certaine Wytches at Chensforde in the Countie of Essex*. London: William Pickering, 1566.

Pihlajamäki, Heikki. "'Swimming the Witch, Pricking for the Devil's Mark': Ordeals in the Early Modern Witchcraft Trials." *Journal of Legal History* 21:2 (2000), 35–58.

Potts, Thomas. *The Wonderfull Discoverie of Witches in the Countie of Lancaster*. London: John Barnes, 1613.

Prosperi, Adriano. *Crime and Forgiveness: Christianizing Execution in Medieval Europe*. Trans. Jeremy Carden. Cambridge: Harvard University Press, 2020.

Purkiss, Diane. *The Witch in History: Early Modern and Twentieth-Century Representations*. New York: Routledge, 1996.

Quensel, Stephan. *Witch Politics in Early Modern Europe (1400–1800)*. Wiesbaden: Springer, 2023.

Rémy, Nicolas. *Daemonolatreiae libri tres*. Lyon: Vincentii, 1595.

Demonolatry. Trans. E. Allen Ashwin. Ed. Montague Summers. London: John Rodker, 1930.

A Rehearsall Both Straung and True, of Hainous and Horrible Actes Committed by Elizabeth Stile. London: Edward White, 1579.

Roper, Lyndal. *Oedipus and the Devil: Witchcraft, Sexuality, and Religion in Early Modern Europe*. London: Routledge, 1994.

Witch Craze: Terror and Fantasy in Baroque Germany. New Haven: Yale University Press, 2004.

Rosoni, Isabella. *Quae singula non prosunt collecta iuvant: La teoria della prova indiziaria nel'età medievale e moderna*. Milan: Giuffrè, 1995.

Rowlands, Alison. *Witchcraft Narratives in Germany: Rothenburg 1561–1652*. Manchester: Manchester University Press, Palgrave, 2003.

Schlaefli, Louis. *Les procès de sorcellerie dans la région de Molsheim aux XVIe et XVIIe siècles*. Molsheim: SHAME, 2021.

Scot, Reginald. *The Discoverie of Witchcraft*. London: William Brome, 1584.

Shapiro, Barbara J. *"Beyond Reasonable Doubt" and "Probable Cause": Historical Perspectives on the Anglo-American Law of Evidence*. Berkeley: University of California Press, 1991.

"Classical Rhetoric and the English Law of Evidence." In *Rhetoric and Law in Early Modern Europe*. Ed. Victoria Kahn and Lorna Hutson. New Haven: Yale University Press, 2001, 54–72.

Probability and Certainty in Seventeenth-Century England: A Study of the Relationships Between Natural Science, Religion, History, Law, and Literature. Princeton: Princeton University Press, 1983.

Sharpe, James. *The Bewitching of Anne Gunter: A Horrible and True Story of Deception, Witchcraft, Murder, and the King of England*. New York: Routledge, 2000.

Witchcraft in Early Modern England. 2nd ed. New York: Routledge, 2020.

"Women, Witchcraft and the Legal Process." In *Women, Crime and the Courts in Early Modern England*. Ed. Jennifer Kermode and Garthine Walker. Chapel Hill: University of North Carolina Press, 1995, 106–24.

Smith, Sir Thomas. *The Common-Welth of England*. London: Gregory Seton, 1589.

De republica Anglorum. London: Gregorie Seton, 1583.

Stephens, Walter. *Demon Lovers: Witchcraft, Sex, and the Crisis of Belief*. Chicago: University of Chicago Press, 2002.

"The Sceptical Tradition." In *Oxford Handbook of Witchcraft in Early Modern Europe and Colonial America*. Ed. Brian P. Levack. Oxford: Oxford University Press, 2013, 101–21.

Stern, Laura Ikins. *The Criminal Law System of Medieval and Renaissance Florence*. Baltimore: Johns Hopkins University Press, 1994.

Swan, John. *A True and Breife Report, of Mary Glovers Vexation*. [London?: s.n.], 1603.

Syme, Holger Schott. *Theatre and Testimony in Shakespeare's England: A Culture of Mediation*. Cambridge: Cambridge University Press, 2012.

The Triall of Maist. Dorrell. [Middelburg: R. Schilders], 1599.

A Tryal of Witches at the Assizes Held at Bury St. Edmonds. London: William Shrewsbery, 1682.

Waardt, Hans de. "Witchcraft and Wealth: The Case of the Netherlands." In *Oxford Handbook of Witchcraft in Early Modern Europe and Colonial America*. Ed. Brian P. Levack. Oxford: Oxford University Press, 2013, 232–48.

The Witches of Northampton-Shire: Agnes Browne. Joane Vaughan. Arthur Bill. Hellen Jenkenson. Mary Barber. London: Arthur Johnson, 1612.

Witmore, Michael. *Pretty Creatures: Children and Fiction in the English Renaissance*. Ithaca: Cornell University Press, 2007.

A World of Wonders. A Masse of Murthers. A Covie of Cosonages. London: William Barley, 1595.

Acknowledgments

I am grateful to Sofia Riva for research assistance, to Marion Gibson and the anonymous reviewers' reports for invaluable suggestions, to Adam Hooper of Cambridge University Press and Vibhu Prathima Palanisame of Integra for easing the publication process, to Malcolm Gaskill for a generous and insightful reading, to Eleanor Johnson for ongoing conversations about the longer history of witchcraft and horror, and to Jesús Velasco and the participants in his fall 2023 colloquium on "The Craft" for exchanges that will continue to inspire me far into the future. As always, my greatest debt is to Nathaniel Berman and Kaia Berman Peters, whose power of enchantment I discover anew every day.

Magic

Series Editor

Marion Gibson

University of Exeter

Marion Gibson is Professor of Renaissance and Magical Literatures and Director of the Flexible Combined Honours Programme at the University of Exeter. Her publications include *Possession, Puritanism and Print: Darrell, Harsnett, Shakespeare and the Elizabethan Exorcism Controversy* (2006), *Witchcraft Myths in American Culture* (2007), *Imagining the Pagan Past: Gods and Goddesses in Literature and History since the Dark Ages* (2013), *The Arden Shakespeare Dictionary of Shakespeare's Demonology* (with Jo Esra, 2014), *Rediscovering Renaissance Witchcraft* (2017), and *Witchcraft: The Basics* (2018). Her new book, *The Witches of St Osyth: Persecution, Murder and Betrayal in Elizabethan England*, will be published by CUP in 2022.

About the Series

Elements in Magic aims to restore the study of magic, broadly defined, to a central place within culture: one which it occupied for many centuries before being set apart by changing discourses of rationality and meaning. Understood as a continuing and potent force within global civilisation, magical thinking is imaginatively approached here as a cluster of activities, attitudes, beliefs and motivations which include topics such as alchemy, astrology, divination, exorcism, the fantastical, folklore, haunting, supernatural creatures, necromancy, ritual, spirit possession and witchcraft.

Cambridge Elements

Magic

Elements in the Series

A full series listing is available at: www.cambridge.org/EMGI

For EU product safety concerns, contact us at Calle de José Abascal, 56–1°, 28003 Madrid, Spain or eugpsr@cambridge.org.

www.ingramcontent.com/pod-product-compliance
Ingram Content Group UK Ltd.
Pitfield, Milton Keynes, MK11 3LW, UK
UKHW022144080726
473066UK00010B/753

* 9 7 8 1 0 0 9 4 6 9 7 1 5 *